Defender of Martin Luther and Hero of the Reformation

John Frederick

THE MAGNANIMOUS

COMPILED BY DR. GEORG MENTZ

TRANSLATED BY JAMES LANGEBARTELS

Published by Concordia Publishing House
3558 S. Jefferson Ave., St. Louis, MO 63118-3968
1-800-325-3040 • cph.org

This volume was translated from volume 1 of *Beiträge zur neueren Geschichte Thüringens: Johann Friedrich der Grossmütige, 1503–1554. Erster Teil: Johann Friedrich bis zu seinem Regierungsantritt, 1503–1532*, compiled by Dr. Georg Mentz (Jena: Gustav Fischer Publishing House, 1903).

Manufactured in the United States of America

1 2 3 4 5 6 7 8 9 10 27 26 25 24 23 22 21 20 19 18

CONTENTS

Translator's Introduction

This short biography of the first part of the life of John Frederick the Magnanimous was originally prepared in honor of the four hundredth anniversary of John Frederick's birth. It was first published in 1903 and now appears in English several years after the five hundredth anniversary of his birth. The biographer, Georg Mentz (1870–1943), who was a professor in Jena, is able to tell us much about the development of this man, much that explains or at least helps us to understand what happened later in his life. John Frederick had early exposure to Luther's writings and was completely devoted to him. Luther dedicated one of his early writings to young John Frederick. The continuing importance of this Lutheran elector is shown by the anthology recently published about him.[1]

There were three electors of Saxony during Martin Luther's lifetime with whom he worked somewhat closely. Frederick the Wise (1463–1525) was significant for Luther's development as a theological professor and for Luther surviving the legal proceedings against him, which culminated in the decree issued at Worms that Luther was an outlaw. Frederick the Wise saw to it that Luther was kept safe at the Wartburg as long as necessary, before Luther returned to Wittenberg and taught there in public the rest of his life. Frederick the Wise died on May 5, 1525, and Luther preached for his funeral.[2] There are several biographies of Frederick the Wise; most recently, Sam Wellman's *Frederick the Wise: Seen and Unseen Lives of Martin Luther's Protector* was published by Concordia Publishing House (2015).

Frederick never married and had no legal heirs. His younger brother John the Steadfast (1468–1532) succeeded him as elector of Saxony and filled that

1 Volker Leppin, Georg Schmidt, and Sabine Wefers, *Johann Friedrich I: der lutherische Kurfürst* (Heidelberg: Gütersloher Verlagshaus, 2006).

2 "Sermon for the Burial of Elector Frederick the Wise, 1 Thessalonians 4:13–18" (WA 17/1:196–227; LW 56).

position for seven years. John married Sophie of Mecklenburg-Schwerin on March 1, 1500, and their union was blessed with a son born on June 30, 1503. Because this boy would be the heir of both his father and his uncle, he was given both names: John Frederick. Unfortunately, his mother died less than two weeks after he was born. This biography documents how often Frederick shared his rule as elector with his brother, John, and then also how often John involved young John Frederick in the government before John's death on August 16, 1532. There are no satisfactory biographies of John the Steadfast. Carl Franz Anton Jagemann published a biography of John the Steadfast and John Frederick the Magnanimous in 1756,[3] but his writing is long on praise and short on facts. Johannes Becker prepared a doctoral dissertation on Elector John's relationship to Luther, which does not fulfill what might be expected from such a book.[4] Mentz does not mention either of these books in his list of works cited below.

Georg Mentz published this first volume on the early life of John Frederick in time for the anniversary of his birth, but then did much more research for the second and third volumes of his biography. Volume 2 covers the time when John Frederick the Magnanimous served as elector of Saxony during the remainder of Luther's life. Volume 3 covers the time after this, focusing on the Smalcald War with its defeat for John Frederick and his allies at Mühlberg, his imprisonment, and his death. Volumes 2 and 3 are much longer than volume 1, and the translations are not yet completed.

An obvious strength of Mentz's biography is his abundant use of the original documents in the archives, which he footnotes in detail. In addition, he chose some of the documents he found for publication. Over two dozen such documents fill the last pages of this volume, and eighty-two more are included at the end of volume 3. Mentz provides these documents transcribed from the original handwriting but retains the original grammar, spelling, and abbreviations. While these documents are valuable and helpful, the translation furnished here is not necessarily completely accurate. It is the best that can be done but includes many guesses at the meaning. Note that throughout this translation, the original page numbers of Mentz's biography are included within angle brackets.

Perhaps a weakness of Mentz's biography is his tendency to refer to individuals by their office or their relatives. References to "the landgrave" are

---

3 Jagemann, *Kurzgefaßte Lebensbeschreibung der durchlauchtigsten Herzoge und Churfürsten zu Sachsen, Johann des Standhaften und Johann Friedrichs des Großmüthigen, zweyer glorwürdigen Bekenner des Evangelii* (Halle, 1756).

4 Becker, *Kurfürst Johann von Sachsen und seine Beziehungen zu Luther, Teil I. 1520–1528* (Leipzig, 1890).

generally references to Philip, landgrave of Hesse. However, Philip is also referred to repeatedly as John Frederick's cousin, since their mothers, Sophie of Mecklenburg-Schwerin (1481–1503) and Anna of Mecklenburg-Schwerin (1485–1525), were sisters. References to uncles are much harder to pin down.

The following genealogical information will be helpful. Saxony had been divided into Albertine Saxony and Ernestine Saxony, so called because of Ernst (1441–86) and Albert (the Courageous, 1443–1500), the two sons of Frederick II the Gentle (1412–64) and his wife, Margaret of Austria (1416–86). Albert's son is George (duke of Saxony, 1471–1539), referred to often in this book. Ernst and his wife, Elisabeth (1443–84), had two sons of interest to us here, Frederick (the Wise, 1463–1525) and John (the Steadfast, 1468–1532). John and his wife Sophie (1481–1503) had one son, John Frederick; John the Steadfast had other children with his second wife, Margaret (1494–1521).

I extend my thanks to Rev. Paul T. McCain of Concordia Publishing House for his encouragement and guidance on this project.

Preface

The external motive for compiling this book was the approaching celebration on June 30 of the four hundredth birthday of John Frederick the Magnanimous. The Thuringian Historical Commission believed that this day not only deserved to be celebrated by the University of Jena, but that it also should be the occasion for one of the most necessary tasks of Thuringian historical investigation, namely, to set about compiling the history of John Frederick the Magnanimous. Whoever has but paged through the registers of the Ernestine United Archives at Weimar knows what masses of archival records there are for this field, often almost completely unused. He will be convinced that a way through this multitude of official documents can only be found if the person of the elector is made the focus. He can only dare to hope that many new facts and many previously divergent views will result for the influence John Frederick had for two decades on German history and on Reformation history, and also for other fields. How the image of the elector takes shape is academically not important; yet we would certainly expect that the disclosure of authentic materials would provide something of worth about his government. Previously, almost nothing has been known about his activity in the field of administering his land.

Since the author had only a few months available for this, he was not in the position to search into the elector's own time of government; yet, this book will show that a systematic investigation of the materials can still bring to light many interesting things. The author would not have been able to complete even this fragment if his work had not been facilitated by the exceptional kindness of the administrations of the archives and libraries he used in Coburg, Dresden, Gotha, and Weimar, above all by the untiring helpfulness of the officials at the Ernestine United Archives at Weimar. Most sincere thanks to all of these!

The author believed he would be doing a service to other investigators if he attached some of the chief documents as an appendix. Those items were primarily selected that can be regarded as direct, independent statements of John Frederick. The form of the texts is essentially guided by the principles of the third German historical conference, although it was not possible for the author, who only had a short time for the printing, to satisfy all the demands he himself was inclined to make for the publication of official documents, especially with reference to factual and linguistic explanations.

Jena, June 1903

G. Mentz

WORKS CITED BY ABBREVIATION

- Alt. = Altenburg Edition of Luther's Works
- Baumgarten, H., *Geschichte Karls V.*, 3 vols. (Stuttgart, 1885–92)
- Beck, Aug., *Johann Friedrich der Mittlere*, 2 vols. (Weimar, 1858)
- Below, G. v., *Landtagsakten von Jülich-Berg*, vol. 1 (Düsseldorf, 1895)
- Bolte = *Die schöne Magelone*, translated by Veit Warbeck, published by Joh. Bolte (*Bibliothek älterer deutscher Übersetzungen*, vol. 1, published by Aug. Sauer [Weimar, 1894])
- Bouterweck, K. W., *Sibylle, Kurfürstin von Sachsen* in *Zeitschr. des Bergischen Geschichtsvereines*, vol. 7 (Bonn, 1871)
- Burkhardt = *Dr. Martin Luthers Briefwechsel*, published by C. A. H. Burkhardt (Leipzig, 1866)
- Burkhardt, C. A. H., *Ernestinische Landtagsakten*, vol. 1, in *Thüringische Geschichtsquellen* N. F. 5 (Jena, 1902)
- Burkhardt, C. A. H., *Geschichte der sächsischen Kirchen- und Schulvisitationen von 1524–45* (Leipzig, 1879)
- Cordatus, *Tagebuch über M. Luther 1537*, published by H. Wrampelmeyer (Halle, 1885)
- Cornelius = C. A. Cornelius, *Briefwechsel zwischen Herzog Johann Friedrich von Sachsen und Graf Wilhelm von Nuenahr in den Jahren 1529 bis 1536*, in *Zeitschr. des Bergischen Geschichtsvereines*, vols. 10, 14 (Bonn, 1874, 1878)
- CR = *Corpus Reformatorum* (Halle and Braunschweig, 1834f.)
- Cyprian, E. S., *Nützliche Urkunden zur Erläuterung der ersten Reformationsgeschichte*, vols. 1 and 2, in W. E. Tentzel, *Historischer Bericht vom Anfang und ersten Fortgang der Reformation* (Gotha, 1717/18)
- Devrient, E., *Die älteren Ernestiner* (Berlin, 1897)
- Dithmar, *Codex diplomaticus zu Teschenmacher, Annales Cliviae* (Frankfurt and Leipzig, 1721)
- Dommer, A. v., *Die Lutherdrucke der Hamburger Stadtbibliothek* (Leipzig, 1888)

- Droysen, J. G., *Über das Verlöbnis der Infantin Katharina mit Herzog Johann Friedrich von Sachsen 1519*, in the *Berichten der Sächs. Ges. d. Wissensch. Philol.-histor. Kl.*, vol. 5 (1853)
- Ehses, St., *Geschichte der Packschen Händel* (Freiburg i. Br., 1881)
- Enders = *Luthers Briefwechsel*, prepared by E. L. Enders, 8 vols. (Calw and Stuttgart, 1884–98)
- Erl. = *Luthers sämtliche Werke*, Erlangen edition
- Fabricius, G. F., *Origines illustr. Stirpis Saxonicae contin. A. Jac. Fabricio* (Leipzig, 1607)
- Faselius, J. A. L., *Versuch einer kurzen Lebensgeschichte Johann Friedrichs des Großmütigen* (Weißenfels and Leipzig, 1799)
- Ficker, Joh., *Aktenstücke zu den Religionsverhandlungen des Reichstages zu Regensburg 1532*, in *Zeitschr. f. Kirchengesch.*, vol. 12
- Förstemann = C. E. Förstemann, *Neues Urkundenbuch zur Geschichte der evangelischen Kirchen-Reformation*, vol. 1 (Hamburg, 1842)
- Förstemann, *U.* = C. E. Förstemann, *Urkundenbuch zur Geschichte des Reichstages zu Augsburg im Jahre 1530*, vols. 1 and 2 (Halle, 1833, 1835)
- Friedensburg, W., *Der Reichstag zu Speier 1526*, in *Histor. Untersuchung* 5, published by J. Jastrow (Berlin, 1887)
- Friedensburg, W., *Zur Vorgeschichte des Gotha-Torgauischen Bündnisses der Evangelischen* (Marburg, 1884)
- Gillert, *Der Briefwechsel des Conradus Mutianus*, gathered and edited by K. Gillert, in *Geschichtsquellen der Provinz Sachsen*, vol. 18 (Halle, 1890)
- Hain, L., *Repertorium bibliographicum* (Stuttgart and Tübingen, 1826–28)
- Hoffmann, E., *Naumburg a. S. im Zeitalter der Reformation* in *Leipziger Studien a. d. Gebiete der Geschichte*, 7.1 (Leipzig, 1900)
- Hortleder, Fr., *Handlungen und Ausschreiben von den Ursachen des deutschen Krieges* (Frankfurt a. M., 1617)
- Jöcher, *Gelehrtenlexikon*
- Kalkoff, P., *Die Depeschen des Nuntius Aleander vom Wormser Reichstage 1521* (2nd ed., Halle a. S., 1897)

- Kapp, J. E., *Kleine Nachlese einiger zur Erläuterung der Reformationsgeschichte nützlicher Urkunden*, vols. 1–4 (Leipzig, 1727–33)
- Kawerau, G., *Der Briefwechsel des Justus Jonas*, vols. 1 and 2, in *Geschichtsquellen der Prov. Sachsen* 17 (Halle, 1884f.)
- Kius, O[tto], *Das Finanzwesen des Ernestinischen Hauses Sachsen im sechszehnten Jahrhundert* (Weimar, 1863)
- Kolde = Th. Kolde, *Friedrich der Weise und die Anfänge der Reformation* (Erlangen, 1881)
- Köstlin, Julius, *Martin Luther*, vol. 1, continued by G. Kawerau (5th ed., Berlin, 1903)
- Krause, C., *Euricius Cordus* (Marburg, 1863)
- Kronfeld, J. C., *Landeskunde des Großherzogtums Sachsen-Weimar-Eisenach*, 2 vols. (Weimar, 1878/79)
- Laemmer, H., *Monumenta Vaticana* (Freiburg, 1861)
- Lanz, K., *Korrespondenz des Kaisers Karl V.*, 3 vols. (Leipzig, 1844–46)
- Lenz, M., *Briefwechsel Landgraf Philipps des Großmütigen mit Luther*, published by M. Lenz, 3 vols. (Leipzig: Prussian State Archives, 1880, 1887, 1891)
- Lenz, M., *Kritische Erörterungen zur Wartburgszeit* (Marburg, 1883)
- Lenz, M., *Zwingli und Landgraf Philipp* in *Zeitschr. F. Kirchengesch.* 3
- Lith, J. W. v. d., *Erläuterung der Reformationshistorie* (Schwobach, 1733)
- Loesche, G., *Analecta Lutherana et Melanthoniana* (Gotha, 1892)
- Luther, M., *Tischreden*, published by K. E. Förstemann, 4 vols. (Leipzig and Berlin, 1844–48)
- LW = Luther's Works, American Edition, 75 vols. (St. Louis: Concordia, and Philadelphia: Muhlenberg and Fortress, 1955–)
- Meinardus, O., *Der Katzenelnbogische Erbfolgestreit*, vol. 1, parts 1 and 2, in *Nassau-Oranische Korrespondenzen*, vol. 1 (Wiesbaden, 1898)
- Müller, J., *Quellenschriften und Geschichte des deutschsprachlichen Unterrichts bis 1550*, an appendix to C. Kehr, *Geschichte der Methodik des deutschen Volksschulunterrichts*, vol. 4 (Gotha, 1882)

- Müller, J. G., *Jugendliche Geschichte Johann Friedrichs des Großmütigen* (Jena, 1765)
- Müller, J. J., *Historie von der evangelischen Stände Protestation und Augsburgischen Confession* (Jena, 1705)
- Müller, J. S., *Des Hauses Sachsen Annales* (Weimar, 1700)
- Myconius, F., *Historia reformationis*, published by Cyprian (2nd ed., Leipzig, 1718)
- Neudecker, Chr. G., *Merkwürdige Aktenstücke aus dem Zeitalter der Reformation*, vols. 1 and 2 (Nuremberg, 1838)
- Neudecker, Chr. G., and Preller, L., *Spalatins historischer Nachlaß und Briefe. I. Friedrichs des Weisen Leben und Zeitgeschichte* (Jena, 1851)
- Ney, J., *Geschichte des Reichstags zu Speier im Jahre 1529*, in *Mitteilungen des Historischen Vereins der Pfalz.*, vol. 8 (Speyer, 1879)
- Noack, Fr., *Die Exception Sachsens von der Wahl Ferdinands I* (Krefeld, 1886)
- Oergel, *Briefwechsel Erfurtischer Gelehrter aus der Zeit des Humanismus und der Reformation*, in *Mitteilungen des Vereins für d. Gesch. u. Altertumsk. von Erfurt*, No. 15 (Erfurt, 1892)
- PC = *Politische Correspondenz der Stadt Straßburg im Zeitalter der Reformation.* Volume 1 compiled by H. Virek; Volume 2 compiled by O. Winckelmann (Straßburg, 1882–87)
- Planitz, H. v. d., *Berichte aus dem Reichsregiment in Nürnberg 1521–23.* Assembled by E. Wülcker, compiled by H. Virek. *Schriften der sächs. Kommiss. f. Gesch.* 3 (Leipzig, 1899)
- Posse, O., *Die Wettiner. Genealogie des Gesamthauses Wettin* (Leipzig and Berlin, 1897)
- Ranke, *Deutsche Geschichte*, vols. 1–6, 4th ed.; in the *Sämtlichen Werken*, vols. 1–6 (Leipzig, 1867–68)
- Ritter, M., *Sachsen und der Jülicher Erbfolgestreit* (Paper of the Munich Academy, 1873)
- Rommel, Chr. V., *Philipp der Großmütige*, vols. 1–3 (Gießen, 1830)
- RTA = *Deutsche Reichstagsakten. Jüngere Reihe*, vols. 1–3 (Gotha, 1893, 1896, 1901)

- Schade, O., *Satiren und Pasquille aus der Reformationszeit*, 3 vols. (Hannover, 1856–58)
- Scheurl, Chr., *Briefbuch*, vols. 1 and 2, published by F. von Soden and J. K. F. Knaake (Potsdam, 1867, 1872)
- Schirrmacher, F. W., *Briefe und Akten zu der Gesch. des Religionsgespräches zu Marburg 1529 und des Reichstages zu Augsburg 1530* (Gotha, 1876)
- Schlegel, Chr., *Historia Vitae Georgii Spalatini* (Jena, 1693)
- Schöppe, *Zur Geschichte der Reformation in Naumburg* (*Neue Mitteilungen auf dem Gebiete histor.-antiquar. Forschungen* 20 [1900])
- Schornbaum, K., *Die Stellung des Markgrafen Casimir von Brandenburg zur reformatorischen Bewegung* (Erl. Diss. Nuremberg, 1900)
- Schwarz, Hilar, *Landgraf Philipp von Hessen und die Packschen Händel* (*Historische Studien* 13 [Leipzig, 1884])
- Seckendorf, V. L. v., *Commentarius de Lutheranismo*, vols. 1–3 (folio, Frankfurt and Leipzig, 1692)
- Seelheim, Ad., *Georg Spalatin als sächsischer Historiograph* (Halle, 1876)
- Sleidan, Jo., *De statu religionis et rei publicae commentarii* (1558)
- Spalatin, G., *Annales reformationis oder Jahrbücher von der Reformation Lutheri*. Published by E. S. Cyprian (Leipzig, 1718)
- Spalatin ap. Menck = Spalatin, *Annales und Vitae aliquot Electorum*, in *J. B. Menckenii Scriptores Rerum Germanicarum*, vol. 2 (Leipzig, 1728)
- StL = *Dr. Martin Luthers Sämmtliche Schriften*. Edited by Albrecht F. Hoppe. 23 vols. (St. Louis, 1880–1910)
- Stoy, St., *Erste Bündnisbestrebungen evangelischer Stände* (*Ztschr. des Vereins für thür. Gesch.* N. F. 6 [1888])
- Struve, B. G., *Neu eröffnetes historisch und politisches Archiv*, vols. 1–3 (Jena, 1718–19)
- Stumpf, A. S., *Baierns politische Geschichte*, vol. 1 with an index (Munich, 1816)
- WA = *D. Martin Luthers Werke: Kritische Gesamtausgabe*. 73 vols. in 85 (Weimar, 1883–)

- WA Br = *D. Martin Luthers Werke: Briefwechsel.* 18 vols. (Weimar, 1930–)
- WA DB = *D. Martin Luthers Werke: Deutsche Bibel.* 12 vols. in 15 (Weimar, 1906–)
- Weller, E., *Repertorium typographicum* (= G. W. Panzer, *Annalen*, vol. 3) (Nördlingen, 1864)
- Wette, de = *Martin Luthers Briefe, Sendschreiben und Bedenken*, vols. 1–5 compiled by W. M. L. de Wette; vol. 6 compiled by J. K. Seidemann (Berlin, 1825–28, 1856)
- Wette, G. A. de, *Historische Nachrichten von Weimar* (Weimar, 1737–39)
- Wilhelm, Lorenz, *Beschreibung der Stadt Zwickau* (Zwickau, 1633)
- Wille, J., *Philipp der Großmütige von Hessen und die Restitution Ulrichs von Wirtemberg 1526–35* (Tübingen, 1882)
- Winckelmann, O., *Der Schmalkaldische Bund 1530–1532 und der Nürnberger Religionsfriede* (Straßburg, 1892)

OTHER ABBREVIATIONS

All citations beginning with "Loc." come from the Royal Saxon State Archives in Dresden. All citations beginning with "Reg." come from the Saxon-Ernestine United Archives in Weimar.

<1> Chapter 1

YOUTH, EDUCATION, MARRIAGE

PARENTAGE AND EARLY YOUTH

We might wonder why the Hohenzollerns and not the Wettins gained the ascendancy in North Germany. Elector Albert III Achilles (1414–86) of Brandenburg, in his last will and testament in 1473, had set definite limits in the *Dispositio Achillea* on the possibility of dividing the Hohenzollern estates. Twelve years later, the Wettins Ernst and Albrecht, after twenty-four years of joint rule, decided, against the testamentary stipulations of their father, to divide their estates between them. Unlike previous similar cases in which the estates were destined to be reunited, this division became permanent. They did not form two regions, each of which was capable of an independent existence, but both lines retained an interest in all the property of the house. The result was a scissor-shaped structure in which there could be no lack of friction between the two parts. The absurdity of this division is shown by the intricate configuration of the borders brought about by the members of the estate. This, in fact, only served to produce an ever-increasing hostility between both lines during the next decades, which finally led in the Smalcald War to a forced adjustment in favor of the younger Albertine line. Their ancestor Albert <2> the Courageous[1] had already possessed the correct political judgment that every further division of his house would mean a further weakening of it and so issued a law of succession, which should have thwarted such a division. In the Ernestine line, it would still be centuries before they advanced to such great political wisdom. After the death of Ernst,[2] founder of the older line, his two sons Frederick and John avoided dividing the inheritance between them.[3] The reason

1 That is, the founder of the Albertine line, Albert the Courageous (1443–1500), brother of Ernst.—Tr.

2 Albert's older brother Ernst (1441–86) was elector of Saxony 1464–86.—Tr.

3 Frederick III (the Wise, 1463–1525) was elector of Saxony 1486–1525. He never married but maintained a long-standing relationship with Anna Weller. His brother John the Steadfast (1468–1532) was elector of Saxony 1525–32.—Tr.

Frederick the Wise decided to give up conjugal bliss for himself is possibly to be sought not only in disappointed hopes or in his love for Anna Weller, but also in the judgment that a further splintering of the territory and authority by establishing two lines was unavoidable. Since he left the propagation of the house to his brother John, we can imagine what great joy there was in the court at Torgau when a son was born on June 30, 1503, to John, who had married several years earlier.[4] When the boy's mother, Sophie of Mecklenburg, died on July 12 of the same year,[5] the future of the Ernestine house depended for several years on this baby.

At his Baptism, they conferred on the prince the double name of John Frederick; it is possible that they were expressing in this way that in a certain sense, he had two fathers and so was appointed to be the heir both of his father, John, and of his uncle Frederick.[6] People certainly found more of his father than of his uncle in him. When he excelled in stubbornness and obstinacy, and even when he was not completely free from fits of rage, he perhaps had inherited this from his mother. Even though next to nothing has been handed down about her,[7] she was the sister of an Anna of Hesse and a Catharine of Saxony.[8] Any personal influence of Sophie on her son was of course made impossible by her early death, and so he received an essentially masculine education. Even though the persons who <3> stood sponsor at his Baptism—governor of Saxony Heinrich Leser, Pastor Koberger of Torgau, and Anna Metzsch, the widow of Kaspar Metzsch[9]—could suggest a certain civic simplicity in John's household, it was, on the other hand, regarded as necessary to establish at once a kind of court for the young prince. A nobleman, Ernst von Isserstedt,[10] was appointed his private tutor; a servant, Dietz (a woman), and a nanny waited on him; and the nurse, Barbara, met the boy's need for nourishment.[11] It emerges from some surviving invoices that an especially detailed account was kept of

---

4 Posse, *Die Wettiner*, Table 7, No. 9.

5 Posse, *Die Wettiner*, Table 7, No. 6. John had married Sophie of Mecklenburg-Schwerin (1481–1503) on March 1, 1500.

6 This later gave rise to all kinds of poetic and philosophical reflections; cf. Euricius Cordus, *Epigrammata*, book 6, 185.

7 Berbig, *Die Gemahlinnen der Regenten des gothaischen Landes*, 8f., which also includes her picture.

8 Anna (1485–1525) ruled Hesse for ten years and was the mother of Landgrave Philip of Hesse (1504–67). Catharine (1487–1561) was instrumental in introducing the Reformation to Freiburg and Dresden.—Tr.

9 Goth. Bibl. Cod. chart, fol. 52, Bl. 287; J. G. Müller, *Jugendliche Geschichte Johann Friedrichs*, 7.

10 The official documents spell this Eysserstädt. Since there was a Bavarian family Eiserstetten, from which an Ernst from Isserstedt was born in 1483 (Kronfeld, *Landeskunde*, 2:272), he is certainly meant. (I am indebted to Dr. Gritzner in Weimar for this reference.)

11 Reg. Bb. 4185, 4188.

expenditures on the apartment or "ladies" of the young lord.[12] Apparently, he spent his early years in Torgau and Lochau and did not join in the frequent journeys of his father. In 1508, he was presented in Wittenberg. There was no lack of flattering greetings for the future sovereign, but we can take scarcely anything definite about John Frederick's life and outward appearance then from the stirring Latin verses of Sibutius.[13]

EDUCATION: SPALATIN

Both Frederick the Wise and John placed a high value on education and expressed this by founding the University of Wittenberg; they naturally desired to give the heir of their nation a classical education. The elector—who occasionally in letters to John calls the prince "our son" or "Your Grace's and my son"[14]—made it his business to choose a suitable teacher. They intended from the start <4> to take into account the new, humanistic education, and so turned to the notable Mutian Rufus in Gotha for advice. He happily reported to Herebord von der Marthen in the fall of 1508 that among many candidates, the one Herebord recommended, Spalatin, carried off the victory. For himself and his whole circle, he attached the most radiant hopes on this promotion of his friend. Spalatin was himself less convinced and was reluctant to exchange the quiet rustic retreat of Georgenthal for the dangerous ground of the court; urgent admonitions from his old friend were required to get him to decide to take up this position.[15] He seems to have gone to the court around Michaelmas 1508, but he began the instruction of the prince first in 1509.[16] For pay, he was offered twenty florins a year, plus new clothes twice a year. Six boys from the nobility were to be educated with the prince. For now, only one of them, Wolf von Hirschfeld, had been named,[17] but it is a safe assumption that many of the later very influential councilors and friends of John Frederick had already spent their youth with him.[18] Unfortunately, we do not know very much about Spalatin's method of education. When Mutian busied himself with pedagogics and asked Herebord in the letter mentioned above for the fables of Laurencius

12 Reg. Bb. 5138, 5139.

13 *Ad illustriss. Saxoniae Principem, magnificentis. Ducis Ioannis filium pro primo suo adventu in urbem Albiorenam Georgii Sibuti . . . carmen et deprecatorium pro prospera valetudine* (Wittenberg, 1508).

14 E.g., Förstemann 1:4; RTA 1:676.

15 *Mutians Briefwechsel*, edited by Gillert 1:147f.

16 According to his own report (Reg. O, No. 155 for the year 1509).

17 Cf. G. v. Hirschfeld in the *Beiträgen zur sächs. Kirchengesch.* 2:154, according to the manuscript of Spalatin in the Weimar Library, fol. 219, 35/36, 170.

18 Cf. also pp. 26–27 <12>.

Abstemius[19] and for Plutarch's book on the education of children,[20] it is a safe assumption that he wanted to support the young educator with his council. At any rate, he was interested in Spalatin's further activity and cheerfully reported on January 17, 1509, about the excellent impression he made at court.[21] Soon, however, he had to contend with a dangerous discontent that overcame his friend. Spalatin was not as pleased with the court as the court was with him; he did not feel he was in his element there; he seemed to be an exile; <5> bodily ailments were added to this; above all, he did not find the contentment he desired in his actual assignment. He did not have an entirely free hand in his work of education. He soon fell into disagreements with the old private tutor of the prince, which in any case we see as referring to no one other than Ernst von Isserstedt. Ernst may have been a somewhat stubborn and pedantic man who perhaps belonged to the faction at court that despised the scholars and the clergy; Spalatin, however, bore a large part of the blame for the conflict, which seems to have led to an almost complete rupture already in 1509. He was beating his head against a wall trying to make his pupils into young scholars without regard for their future tasks. Mutian and Urban were right to explain to him in their letters that aristocratic boys not only had to learn Latin and ethics, but also the behavior corresponding to their position; for teacher and for students, recreation and movement outside, in between work, was beneficial. If Spalatin adhered to the principles he had followed so far, it would not be surprising if the boys would feel more drawn to the private tutor, who even once laughed in their presence, than to him.[22]

These admonitions do not seem to have had complete success; Mutian had to come to court himself to look after things. He found Spalatin miserable. Although John Frederick made an excellent impression on him, he found the private tutor to be an honest but somewhat grumpy man, averse to the arts. The brother princes, however, greatly appreciated his suggestions. Frederick the Wise intended to send his nephew to Wittenberg, where Spalatin could study together with him.[23] Nothing came of this; in 1510, we find teacher and students in Eisenach.[24]

Spalatin seems gradually to have reached a more peaceful state of mind, or he would not have held out until the fall of 1511. In general, people envied him

---

19 Cf. Hain, *Rep. bibl.*, No. 26. (That is, *Hecatomythium* [1495].—Tr.)

20 *De liberis educandis.* Hain, No. 13134.

21 Gillert 1:164f.

22 Gillert 1:168f., 228.

23 Gillert 1:253.

24 Gillert 2:365. On Spalatin's educational work, cf. Seelheim, *Georg Spalatin als sächs. Historiograph*, 15f.

for his position <6> and John Frederick for his teacher.[25] John Frederick later expressed his regret that he did not have the benefit of Spalatin's instruction longer.[26] Unfortunately, we cannot say much of anything about the nature of this instruction, beyond what has already been said about externals. Only one book purchase for the prince falls into the time of Spalatin's educational activity: at Easter 1511, in Leipzig, a *Garden of the Soul*[27] was purchased, certainly for religious instruction.

On the whole, however, it became more and more obvious that Spalatin was not suited to be occupied with such elementary things as the instruction of an eight-year-old boy, even if there was the best hope for him.[28] Since 1510, he had at the direction of the elector been active in historical matters[29] and had translated Latin documents for him. When in the fall of 1511, nephews of the elector Otto and Ernst of Lüneburg[30] entered the University of Wittenberg, it appeared to be an opportune way out of all difficulties to send Spalatin as their guide. "It had turned out that the young prince was still too young for Spalatin's kind of education."[31] We can only accept this as the reason for Spalatin's departure, for even if on May 29, 1512, he was still complaining about the enemies of the arts at the court,[32] we have no satisfactory proof to accept that he had to yield to the faction of nobles who did not want the young count to learn too much. On the contrary, it is not impossible that the final outcome of the conflicts between Spalatin and Isserstedt is referred to in a statement of Luther in his Table Talks.[33] This cannot be referring to a victory by the enemies of the arts, because the education of John Frederick was carried on completely in the same way. Of course, <7> it was not very easy to find a suitable replacement for Spalatin. His successor, Kaspar Lichtem (?), was replaced in the same year by Kaspar Rot from Oelsnitz. He also, however, appears not to have met with approval, and in 1512, they found someone who would work: Alexius Krosner from Colditz, who, according to the custom of that time, was called Colditius.[34]

---

25 Scheurl, *Briefbuch,* 1:65, 76f.

26 Cordatus, *Tagebuch,* No. 1609.

27 *Hortulus animae,* Reg. Bb. 4212.

28 In an April 29, 1512, letter to Lang, Spalatin called the prince *optimae spei principem,* "a prince of the best hope" (Goth. Bibl. Cod. chart. A 399, fol. 272f.).

29 Reg. O, No. 155.

30 Frederick's sister Margarete (1469–1528) married Henry I of Lüneburg (1468–1532); Otto (1495–1549) and Ernst (1497–1546) were two of their children.—Tr.

31 Scheurl, *Briefbuch,* 1:80.

32 In the letter to Lang. (The letter quoted earlier in this paragraph is dated April 29, 1512, not May 29, 1512.—Tr.)

33 Cordatus, No. 671, 1609; Förstemann, *Luthers Tischreden,* 4:474.

34 According to a note found in Neudecker's literary remains in the Goth. Bibl. Cod. chart A 1289, 2 fol. 85.

It was one of the Kaspars who brought it about that on November 29, 1511, the twelve books of Donatus,[35] a Remigius,[36] and an Alexander[37] were purchased for the prince.[38] Thus the Latin instruction probably begun by Spalatin was enthusiastically pursued. Our sources are more plentiful after Krosner began his activity.[39] He seems not to have had to contend with the same difficulties Spalatin had, for on November 27, 1511, Isserstedt had been pensioned with an annual allowance of thirty florins and two sacks of grain.[40] His successor as private tutor, Heinrich von Bünau,[41] appears to have let the new educator do as he liked.

EDUCATION: KROSNER

Krosner also had received a classical education and, at the start, seems to have set a high goal. The poems he directed to the prince in 1513 made very little allowance for his youth. The reasons with which he sought to convince him of the necessity of learning Greek will scarcely have made a strong impression on the boy.[42] For all that, they did courageously begin with Greek, as John Frederick's exercise book preserved to us from 1513 shows.[43] <8> The demands the teacher made on his pupil were of course very small. After the prince had written down the Greek alphabet with some Latin explanations on the length of the vowels, he went on to record some Ἀποφτέγματα[44] τῶν Ἑλλήνων in the Greek, Latin, and German languages. This is followed by a brief section on the accents, and then it already says τέλος τῶν γράμματον ελλήνον (!).[45] This is then followed as a further exercise by the Our Father and the Ave Maria in Greek and Latin. John Frederick would scarcely have had all that much use for these "*Rudimenta Graecanica*"!

The second part of his exercise book contains a collection of German and Latin aphorisms. In these "witty sayings gathered from many Latin authors,"

35 Certainly the *Ars grammatica*, which of course only has three books.

36 Either Remigius's *per figurae* or the *Regulae*; cf. Hain, *Repertorium*, No. 13855f.; J. Müller, *Quellenschriften*, 259.

37 Probably Alexander, *de Villa Dei*; cf. Köstlin, *Luther*, 1:36.

38 Reg. Bb. 4214.

39 On his earlier history, cf. Bauch in *Zeitschr. f. Kirchengesh.*, 18:402.

40 Reg. Bb. 4215, 4223; he was still receiving this annual allowance in 1520.

41 First mentioned in December 1513 at an annual pay of fifty florins (Reg. Bb. 4238).

42 Printed in J. G. Müller's *Jugendl. Gesch.*, 35–38.

43 Weim. Bibl. Msc. Q. 13[d].

44 That is, ἀποφθέγματα, terse sayings in Greek; it is uncertain who is responsible for this spelling mistake.—Tr.

45 That is, "The end of Greek grammar," with several spelling mistakes.—Tr.

the old Greeks and Romans, Church Fathers and humanists are peacefully side by side, Jerome next to Eusebius and Bebelius,[46] Colditius and John Frederick next to Solon and Terence. John Frederick saw himself in the aphorisms: *Virtus et ars praecellit omnes gemmas et aurum*, "Virtue and skill are more valuable than all jewels and gold," and *Foelices omnes homines, qui humiles sunt*, "Blessed are all people who are humble." In other respects, the choice of aphorisms points unmistakably to the future calling of the prince; even in the midst of Greek grammar, this statement is found: "A prince and nobleman should never forget honorable and honest actions, whether he is eating or playing, but should always either himself do something great or remember those who have done honest things."[47]

The instruction seems later to have been limited to the treatment of a single author, and this could scarcely be anyone other than Terence. The prince must first write down Terence's life, then a brief essay on what comedy is, and, finally, the plot of Terence's play *Andria* in German. This concluded the lectures on this point, for under the heading, "Thoughts and words gathered from Terence," we find a kind of worksheet or collection of phrases from *Andria*.

From Terence, they went on to Curtius Rufus.[48] From his sixth book, John Frederick copied down the embassy of the Scythians to Alexander the Great asking him to stop making war on them, provided it with all kinds of comments, and translated it into German.

<9> The next step was thirty-three fables of Aesop in the translation of Laurentius Valla.[49] Finally, the conclusion of the exercise book was formed by the prince's Latin confession, in which he lined up the five senses, the seven deadly sins, and the Ten Commandments in the German language.

All we have analyzed in this booklet is very interesting; however, since Colditz was active as the teacher of John Frederick until 1519, this booklet would be somewhat scanty if we had to regard it as the outcome of all his instruction. We are happy, therefore, to refer to a second official document, which reveals to us a more delightful view of the training the prince received. When Colditz left his position with John Frederick in 1519, an inventory was taken of all the

46 That is, Heinrich Bebel (1472–1518), a humanist known for his *Facetiae* (1508), a collection of anecdotes. Instead of Eusebius, the text has Busebius, an obvious misprint.—Tr.

47 That is, *Ain furst und edel mensch sal nummer vergessen rumlicher und redlicher thate, es esse odir spil, sonder sal alezeit enczwar selbst eczwas grosses thun odir der ihenen gedencken, die Redlich that gethan haben.*—Tr.

48 That is, Quintus Curtius Rufus (first century AD), author of *Historiae Alexandri Magni*, originally in ten books.—Tr.

49 Hain, No. 320–23.

treasures, clothes, and other property of the prince.[50] In it, we also have a list of the books that were then found in his possession; he had at his disposal nineteen Latin and eighteen German books. Numbered among these were also an "Apprenticeship of the Best Prince,"[51] written by the prince himself, and the already mentioned *Rudimenta Graecanica*. We should regard the "Grammatical Rules for Latin and Greek prepared by Alexius Krosner Colditz," the "Principles of a Prince," and the "Vocabulary" more as copy-books than as books. Terence is represented by a large and a small edition; the list next specifies *The Education of a Christian Prince* by Erasmus, the letters of Libanius, the *Instruction* of Aldus, and the grammar of Brassicanus. On the other hand, it appears that Donatus, Remigius, and Alexander had in the meantime gone missing. Among the German books, the first place was taken by *The Rule for Princes*, and then Livy and Terence in German translation; the other interests of the prince are revealed by Vegecius's book on military science, "Parzival,"[52] a collection of heroic poems, a Turkish chronicle, and a book on fighting. All the other books are religious, and we will take them up later.

Nevertheless, this list does not exhaust the number of books that passed through the hands of the prince, since <10> a Tristan was purchased for him at Michaelmas 1515;[53] on New Year's Day 1516, in addition to Titus Livy, three almanacs and a German Amandus;[54] at Easter of the same year, a *Textus sententiarum*[55] and a *Rationale divinorum*;[56] and perhaps at the same time,[57] "a book called *The Old Way*, together with confession,"[58] a rosary,[59] and the Polish battle.[60] Already in his youth, John Frederick seems to have had a liking for collecting books, to which he remained faithful all his life; already now, in addition to the classics, we find books that testify to a definite interest in chivalry, current events, and religious edification.

---

50 Reg. D. 148. I have printed this interesting item as No. 1 of the Official Documents, and there I provide the necessary explanations; see p. 97 <95>.

51 That is, *Tirocinium optimi principis*.—Tr.

52 That is, a poem by Wolfram von Eschenbach about an Arthurian knight and his pursuit of the Holy Grail.—Tr.

53 Reg. Bb. 4252. The reading is not completely certain.

54 Perhaps Amadis de Gaula?

55 *Ob sequentiarum textus*? Hain, No. 14682f. (That is, a textbook on those things that follow logically; however, this could also be a reference to Peter Lombard's *Sentences*.—Tr.)

56 Reg. Bb. 4200. Certainly meant is Duranti, *Rationale divinorum officiorum*, Hain, No. 6461f., a handbook on the liturgy.

57 Reg. Bb. 4269.

58 Possibly also a liturgical book.

59 A rosary of our dear lady; which edition is meant cannot be determined.

60 The battle of the king of Poland with those in Moscow on the day of Mary's birth [September 8], 1514 (Weller, No. 851).

Certainly the prince was given the opportunity to learn all kinds of things. Colditz, however, appears not to have possessed great pedagogical abilities—at least his instruction did not leave behind a good impression in the memory of the prince. John Frederick seems to have been of the opinion that the teacher dealt with him too strictly.[61] Colditz received a salary of forty florins annually,[62] along with occasional special gifts.[63] A bachelor of arts worked alongside him for four florins,[64] but I have not been able to ascertain his name. It also cannot be stated with complete certainty whether the instruction of John Frederick was now still being shared by other boys; Hirschfeld, of course, dropped out already in 1513,[65] yet still at New Year's 1514, <11> four sets of pen and ink were purchased by the "boys" of the young lord,[66] and there is often talk about his "friends." The instruction ended at Michaelmas 1519, and Colditz took up the position of canon in Altenburg, which had been assigned to him already in 1516.[67]

OTHER THINGS ABOUT JOHN FREDERICK'S YOUTH

Only a little can be said about the youth of John Frederick, apart from his academic instruction. His father's second marriage to Margaret of Anhalt on November 13, 1513, does not seem to have brought about any great change in his way of life, although we do now often find him in the company of his stepmother. Frederick and John now separated their households; the fixed residence of the prince was moved from Torgau to Weimar. In March 1513, he was still interceding at the court of Frederick the Wise in favor of a defendant from Eisenach.[68] The stay in Weimar was interrupted by frequent journeys, mostly together with his parents; in May 1514, we find the prince in Gotha, in August in Jena while John was at the diet in Altenburg, and in October in Coburg.[69] Shrove Tuesday 1515 was observed in Zwickau,[70] and the court spent almost

61 "He has not earned praise from me" (Cordatus, op. cit., No. 1609).

62 Reg. Bb. 4238, 4280.

63 E.g., twenty florins at his first Mass on June 1, 1517, at Weimar (Reg. Bb. 4268).

64 Reg. Bb. 4238; he also received a gift of ten florins at his first Mass in Zwickau on April 25, 1518 (Reg. Bb. 4277).

65 In March 1513, Hirschfeld's brother, "who was with My Gracious Young Lord," rode with Pfeffinger to the imperial court (Reg. Bb. 4222).

66 Reg. Bb. 4272.

67 Spalatin ap. Menck, 2:592.

68 Gillert 1:328f.

69 Reg. Bb. 5535, 4242, 4229.

70 Lorenz Wilhelm, *Beschreibung der Stadt Zwickau*, 210, corroborated by Reg. Bb. 5538.

the entire year of 1518 there.[71] The year 1516 brought journeys to Jena and into the electorate; in September of this year, John Frederick was probably taken along for the first time to Trockenborn.[72] His father allowed him to come there again in 1517,[73] and several weeks were now spent nearly every fall there and in Hummelshain for hunting. This same goal may have been served by the journeys to Eisenach generally occurring in August. Summer generally brought a visit with Frederick the Wise in Torgau and Lochau, which seldom occurred without a stay of several days in Wittenberg.[74] These frequent journeys, even <12> if the teacher was brought along in a wagon, were not very beneficial for his studies, and yet John Frederick was learning to know the land and people of his future states. We get a small insight into his way of life, habits, and inclinations at this time from a book of expenditures belonging perhaps in 1515 or 1516.[75] In addition to the almost daily alms and "offerings" in the church, we are struck by the frequent presents for girls, students, and so on who had sung for him. We are reminded by this of the anecdote recurring in all the old biographies of John Frederick, according to which, as an eight- or nine-year-old boy, he had such a special liking for catechism instruction in the church that he asked permission of his father to participate in it.[76] We cannot say that this is based on any actual incident.

In this book of expenditures for the thirteen-year-old, gambling plays a not insignificant role; this reminds us of later times. Generally this concerns only two to three groschen, but once while gambling with his parents and with the prince of Anhalt[77] in Pößneck, he lost twelve groschen, and on May 27, 1514, "one florin, sixteen groschen" is entered as gambling losses of the young lord.[78]

With the discharge of Colditz, John Frederick's proper education was obviously over; after this, there is no mention of a teacher for the young lord, but since 1520, his "Einrosser"[79] is entered on the quarterly report. There are Heinrich and Günther von Bünau, Nickel vom Ende, Wolf von Raschkau and Rotha, and after August 1523, also a Witzleben.[80] We could be inclined to see in them the former classmates of the prince, but no proof of this can be

71 Wilhelm, 211f.

72 Reg. Bb. 5545.

73 Reg. Bb. 5547, and Reg. D. 286.

74 All this according to Reg. Bb.

75 Reg. Bb. 4269.

76 Cf., e.g., J. G. Müller, 19f.

77 That is, Wolfgang I (1492–1566).—Tr.

78 Reg. Bb. 5535.

79 That is, a one-horse vehicle; the context calls for a meaning like "riding companions."—Tr.

80 Reg. Bb. 4296, 4297, 4318.

furnished. From now on, they are the constant companions of the prince and generally accompany him on his journeys.

WARBECK

However, even if John Frederick were regarded as grown up, he still had many things to learn. Especially after he became engaged to the Hapsburg Katharine in 1519, it appeared desirable for him also to acquire some knowledge of <13> French. It seems to have been the duty of teacher Veit Warbeck to instruct him in this. After Warbeck received his teaching degree in Paris in 1509, he had come to Wittenberg in 1514.[81] His knowledge of French caught the attention of Frederick the Wise, who had his natural son, Sebastian von Jessen [ca. 1500–1535], instructed by him in this language. In August 1517, Warbeck again left the court and it seems again lived in Wittenberg. In the next years, however, Frederick the Wise repeatedly drew on him for tasks of a political nature, and even took him along to Frankfurt in 1519.[82] From the end of 1519, the teacher was at the court of John the Steadfast,[83] but it cannot be said with complete certainty which position he filled.[84] His relationship to John Frederick was not strictly defined; I could imagine him as a kind of secretary.[85] His salary amounted to forty florins annually.[86] On June 25, 1524, he was discharged,[87] but then seems to have taken a position similar to what he had with the Saxon princes with Prince Franz of Brunswick-Lüneburg.[88] Since he very frequently stayed at the Weimar court, Warbeck continued a close relationship with John Frederick, provided him with references to Spalatin and other scholars, and supplied him with French books.[89] In <14> 1527, perhaps as a wedding present, he also dedicated to him his translation of *Die schöne Magelone*.[90]

81 Cf. Bolte in *Allgemeine Deutsche Biographie* and in the introduction to his edition of *Die schöne Magelone*; Holstein in *Ztschr. f. d. Philol.*, 17:191f.

82 Schlegel, *Vita Spalatini*, 201f.

83 Reg. N. 806; in the quarterly report, he is first mentioned on February 28, 1520 (Reg. Bb. 4296).

84 He calls himself John's chaplain, and in a September 19, 1523, letter, Lang also calls him "the chief chaplain at Weimar" (Goth. Bibl. Cod. chart. B. 26, 12; cf. Örgel, 21); the court chaplain, however, properly speaking was Wolfgang Stein.

85 On December 14, 1523, Jerome Candelphus wrote to him: "You are the inkstand for the illustrious young prince" (Goth. Bibl. Cod. chart. B. 23–25). John was very indefinite when he wrote on December 29, 1526, to the Altenburg chapter that Warbeck "also serves" his son, John Frederick (Spalatin ap. Menck, 2:664).

86 Reg. Bb. 4296.

87 Reg. Bb. 4324.

88 This is indicated in Spalatin's letter to him in Schlegel.

89 Cf. Bolte, xxix; Schlegel, 219.

90 The original manuscript is in the Gotha library (Cod. chart. B. 437, published by Bolte).

People have justly concluded from these later connections that Veit Warbeck also instructed the young prince in French, for we cannot specify where else John Frederick would have learned French. An interesting manuscript from the Coburg library furnishes us as much insight as is possible into the nature of this instruction.[91] The French copy of *Die schöne Magelone*, on which Warbeck based his German translation, is there. There is a word-for-word Latin interlinear translation; notes in the margin call attention to certain characteristic differences between Latin and French; and several times, German is called on to explain things. Instead of a detailed comparison of the manuscript, I venture to assert (but not with certainty) that this interlinear translation comes from Warbeck, and I hypothesize that Warbeck made use of his pupil's knowledge of Latin to lead him into French and that he later dedicated his translation of the work to him on which he had once based his instruction.

OUTCOME OF JOHN FREDERICK'S EDUCATION

If we contemplate the results of John Frederick's academic education, it certainly cannot be denied that this stirred up in him a lively interest in academic things. This came out especially in his liking for books. To be sure, we cannot determine how many of the books he later had were acquired already in his youth, but we have the impression that he let no chance slip by to enlarge his library; especially his numerous French books and manuscripts[92] were generally acquired during the time of Veit Warbeck, who died already in 1534. As a legacy of Philip of Cleves, a great-uncle of his bride,[93] John Frederick was endowed from Jülich with valuable French works. If we are perhaps somewhat justified <15> in using these French books to define the taste of the prince at this time, then we can mention that in addition to religious books of edification and translations of the classics, books of chivalry played a large role.

John Frederick's interest in academic things further came out in the attention he gave already early on to the university in Wittenberg. In 1525, Luther believed that he could find in him a counterpoise at court to the courtiers who were hostile to education, and he was not deceived in this hope.[94]

In addition to theology, the branch of knowledge that especially interested John Frederick already in his youth, as it did Frederick the Wise, was history;

91 4:2.

92 Bolte published a list of them.

93 Philip of Cleves (1467–1505) was a brother of Sibylle's paternal grandfather, John II (1458–1521).—Tr.

94 May 20, 1525, letter from Luther to John Frederick (WA Br 3:501); June 1, 1525, letter from John Frederick to Luther (WA Br 3:521).

most of all, he carefully followed Spalatin's historical activity. Although the improvements Spalatin undertook in his history of Frederick the Wise came at a later time,[95] he was not turned down when he asked John Frederick for information, for example, on genealogical matters.[96] In general, Spalatin regularly corresponded with him.[97] Already in 1520, he dedicated to him his translation of Plutarch's book *How to Tell a Flatterer from a Friend*.[98] Later, it was Warbeck who carried on the communication, but the direct connection of the scholar with his one-time pupil never completely stopped. His letter of December 1, 1526, shows that he was pleased by his interest in academic things: "I am pleased that his heart attends to good literature and character, as is indeed proper for a prince. Would that the good prince would continue loving and honoring character, so that he becomes a great prince."[99]

It is more difficult to form an opinion on John Frederick's knowledge of academic things than on his interest in them. He himself was later not satisfied with it. He certainly did not make much use later of the Latin and the <16> French he had learned. His unusually numerous German letters and memoranda are sometimes rather detailed, but generally written in a good and clear style.

TOURNAMENTS

In all of this, we have dealt with only one side of John Frederick's development, the intellectual. Alongside of this, as the differences between Spalatin and Isserstedt have already shown, there was a physical development. Mutian was completely correct when he expressed his belief that this dare not be neglected; and to many a lord at court, the development of the young prince in running, jousting, and tournaments seemed more important than all of Spalatin's scholarship. John the Steadfast also had a lively interest in these things and certainly saw to it that the education of his son did not neglect these things. Nothing more specific about this kind of training for the prince has been handed down from his earlier youth, except that in 1518, he attended a tournament in Zwickau.[100] From 1521 on, we are better informed. In the

95 Cf. on this Neudecker and Preller, *Spalatins historischer Nachlaß*, passim; Seelheim, 23f., 37, 52.

96 Schlegel, 239, 241f.

97 This is shown, e.g., by his letters to Warbeck on November 29, 1524, and February 21, 1525 (Goth. Bibl. Cod. chart. B. 26, fol. 135, 141).

98 Cf. *Allgemeine Deutsche Biographie* 35:19.

99 Schlegel, 241f.

100 Wilhelm, 212. See also the weapons listed in Official Document No. 1 on p. 97 <95>.

Dresden library, two splendid tournament books have been preserved for us, one from John the Steadfast covering the years 1487–1527 and one from John Frederick covering the years 1521–34. Color pictures show us all the jousts of the prince from those years; we always see the combatants at the moment of decision. Even when the names have not been added, we can always recognize the prince, so that here we can follow his whole chivalrous career. The books begin at Worms in 1521; in fact, it seems from the correspondence of Frederick the Wise and John that the joust planned for the young prince was to have been the main attraction at the diet. Already in January, he took up preparatory exercises with a wooden man;[101] on February 8, he arrived with his father in Worms; and on Shrove Tuesday, the usual jousting took place. This was <17> evidently the first public appearance of John Frederick,[102] and it was certainly significant that it occurred just before the diet assembled. The outcome was very gratifying. John Frederick jousted three times with Anark von Wildenfels. The first time, Anark was unhorsed; the second time, both remained on their horses; and the third time, both were unhorsed.[103] The impression made on the spectators was so good that after the young prince left the field, Charles V asked him to send him his tackle, because he wanted to use it himself. Naturally, he was glad to fulfill the request.[104]

In May, the prince provided himself with new tackle.[105] His horse blanket now had the motto: "My luck runs on stilts." Müller found this same motto and the date 1521 carved on the wall in Naumburg by the prince.[106] Actually, in the four contests John Frederick risked in 1521, he was thrown four times and only gained the victory once. His enthusiasm was not diminished by this; in 1522, he succeeded in only being unhorsed four times and throwing his opponent eight times. From year to year, he seems to have become a more feared combatant. His opponents were mostly Saxon nobility: in 1522, for the first time, Philip of Brunswick, and in 1523, Wolf of Anhalt. The tournament in Saalfeld took an unfortunate turn for him; John Frederick "fell with his horse, broke his leg, and felt this to the end of his life." He regarded this event as important enough to record it in his own handwriting in Spalatin's contemporary

---

101 Förstemann 1:6, 8; Kolde, 43.

102 The young prince did not yet take part in the two tournaments that took place in Weimar in 1519 (Reg. D. 120).

103 Förstemann 1:81 and the tournament book J, 15.

104 Seckendorf, *Historia Lutheranismi supplem.* ad indic. I, No. 39; Förstemann 1:10f., 16; Kolde, 48.

105 Förstemann 1:19.

106 J. G. Müller, title page and 31f. (Cf. Sam Wellman, *Frederick the Wise* [St. Louis: Concordia, 2015], 203.—Tr.)

history.[107] Since 1526, the prince often competed with Philip of Hesse. There were an especially large number of tournaments in 1527; most interesting of them all for the prince was obviously the contest with the "great Bohemian" Bernhard Schneschke or Zschoschkau. When he defeated him, he was spurred on to new enthusiasm, and in 1528, he succeeded not only in staying in the saddle himself, <18> but also in bringing his feared opponent halfway to the ground. In all, we count 146 jousts for John Frederick in the years 1521–34.[108] Naturally, each such joust was at the same time an occasion for neighboring and friendly princes to gather socially and to deal with political questions; the presence of the ladies offered the opportunity for entering into more delicate relationships. For example, in a very official format on November 25, 1522, John Frederick and Wolf von Anhalt invited Prince George[109] and his sons to Naumburg on Shrove Tuesday 1523, for "jousting, racing, tilting, and foreign fencing." Their attendance would be proof of the unity of the house of Saxony; the prince should bring along his wife and his daughters "together with their women and other charming women and girls." George, however, declined because he had to go to the diet at Nuremberg and had too much else to do.[110]

John Frederick was also certainly not lacking in the other chief princely diversion of the time, the hunt. The annual stay in Lochau, Hummelshain, Trockenborn-Wolfersdorf, and Eisenach provided abundant opportunities to pursue it. We are directly told about his participation in a hunt in 1521.[111] In the following year, Elector Frederick had a picture painted of a hunt of John and John Frederick and sent it with a description to Count Palatine Frederick.[112] On the whole, John Frederick rarely spoke in his letters about hunting; John seems to have had more interest in it than he. It perhaps deserves emphasis that he could report to his son on September 23, 1526, from Trockenborn that a woman had seen three bears.[113]

BETROTHAL TO THE HAPSBURG KATHARINE

It is likely that John Frederick's French instruction was begun because of the proposal of a wife who did not have complete mastery of the German language:

107 Neudecker and Preller, 172; cf. also Kolde, 52.
108 *Arch. f. d. sächs. Gesch.* 15:311.
109 That is, George, duke of Saxony (1471–1539), first cousin of John Frederick's father.—Tr.
110 This correspondence is in Loc. 10526.
111 Spalatin ap. Menck, 2:607.
112 Planitz, *Berichte*, 240f.
113 Reg. E. No. 58 I, handwritten original.

<19> Katharine, the sister of Charles V. Veit Warbeck had entered the service of John just at the time when the prospect of this union taking place was real. This was not the first match that had been planned for John Frederick.[114] Already in 1514 and again in 1517, there is reference in the Weimar documents in quite vague terms to a marriage between two still very young people, John Frederick and Sibylle of Jülich-Cleves, his later wife.[115] This plan was looked at more seriously in 1518.[116] The union seemed especially advisable because this was the simplest way to eliminate the feudal controversies between Saxony and Cleves.[117] Emperor Maximilian also took an interest in the matter, and it was presented to the diet at Jülich-Berg.[118] Then suddenly, all of that was out, for a still more promising possibility was revealed.[119] Charles V, who needed the support of Frederick the Wise for his election, believed, since the Saxon elector took no money, that he could perhaps make an impression on him by encouraging the marriage of his sister Katharine with John Frederick; at all events, Margrave Kasimir of Brandenburg and Count Heinrich of Nassau, who would propose this affair "of themselves as good friends," could be confident of Charles's consent.[120] Now, Frederick did not let himself be moved by this to violate the principle of a free election, but both he and John obviously were very happy to hear of these proposals. The election concluded the matter, which was ratified all around in the next years, and nothing more stood in the way of the fulfillment of the marriage. <20> Indeed, it would probably have actually followed, if in Saxony they had not shied away from the costs of a wedding by proxy. The stay of John and his son in Worms and the vague hints in his correspondence with Frederick may also have reference to the question of the wedding. Charles V finally promised that he would send the bride to the bridegroom six months after his return to Spain.[121] But this did not happen. Whether the resistance of the mother, Johanna, was the real reason, or whether the religious opposition that appeared in Worms made the wedding seem less desirable, it is

---

114 I will not enter any further into the details of the French proposals (RTA 1:51, 53, 136, 499, 829, 838; 2:123f.), nor into the would-be plans for the prince to marry Anna of Hungary (RTA 2:241, 417).

115 Reg. D. 58 I.

116 Reg. D. 58 I.

117 Cf. on this Ritter, 3f.

118 RTA 1:121f.; Below 1:87.

119 All of the following, insofar as it is not cited in the other sources, is from J. J. Müller, *Historie der Augsburgischen Confession*, 688–92; he made use of documents in Reg. D. fol. 30, which now no longer appear to be extant; cf. also Droyson, *Verlöbnis*, 174f.

120 Cf. on the first discussions RTA 1:554, 566, 671, 676, 690f., 703, 734, 797; the French instruction continued (ibid.).

121 RTA 2:833, 844.

impossible to say.[122] For years, the Wettin brothers[123] had to be satisfied with empty words and promises, also in other matters.[124] They became a little averse to mentioning the matter.

The first definite statement from which it could be inferred that, in all likelihood, nothing would come of the marriage was transmitted by Planitz to the elector on July 27, 1523.[125] They then learned from Christian of Denmark that Katharine was to marry the king of Portugal.[126] Yet nothing was decided; sometimes it seemed that the Hapsburg side was thinking about using the marriage to win over the Saxons for the choice of Ferdinand as Roman king.[127] Even at the beginning of 1524, the emperor did not yet dare to explain to the elector that his intentions had changed; his representative at the Nuremberg diet, Hannart, was to explain that the emperor would have the marriage completed "as soon as possible," and that only the war with France had so far prevented it.[128] Even the elector at that time did not at all yet intend without more ado to renounce it.[129] He even considered sending an ambassador to the emperor because of the wedding.[130]

<21> In spite of this, people in Saxony were scarcely very surprised when the cancellation of the engagement then followed. Hannart, at the desire of Ferdinand, would have preferred not to have spoken at all about this matter at the diet. When the elector asked him as they were leaving how things were, he pretended that he had first to await news about this from the emperor.[131] He had journeyed to the diet in North Germany with the assignment of dealing with the matter as gently as possible. On May 14, he met with the elector.[132] We do not know the specific content of the news he brought, but he enlarged on the difficulties standing in the way of the union and spent his time on substitute proposals. He alluded to the daughter of the king of Denmark, the daughter of the king of Naples, and the daughter of the king of Poland; the emperor would gladly support the courtship of the prince and also contribute

---

122 On the attitude of the bride, cf. RTA 2:833f.
123 That is, Frederick the Wise and John the Steadfast.—Tr.
124 Planitz, 223f., 313.
125 Planitz, 503.
126 Neudecke and Preller, 61.
127 Friedensburg, *Reichstag zu Speier*, 21.
128 Förstemann 1:143.
129 Neudecker and Preller, 62.
130 Förstemann 1:179.
131 Lanz, *Korrespondenz Karls V*, 1:113f.
132 Spalatin ap. Menck, 2:635.

a large sum of money.[133] Saxony seems to have answered rather bluntly that it really considered the marriage unbroken and that the responsibility for the "divorce" was on the emperor and his sister.[134] On the whole, however, Frederick acted with dignity in the matter, as is shown in his June 4, 1524, letter of comfort to his brother.[135] John seems to have been less calm. We know nothing about the attitude of the bridegroom.[136] It is striking that Veit Warbeck was dismissed just on June 25, 1524. Did they now suddenly regard French instruction as unprofitable?

In other respects, the marriage question was not allowed to rest. There are some mysterious memoranda from August 1524, which seem to suggest that now King Ferdinand had an interest in the union.[137] Balthasar Wolf von Wolfsthal was at that time commissioned to negotiate with the elector.[138] In Saxony, people probably still thought about the possibility of the marriage for a time; <22> only when they learned in November 1524 that the sister of the emperor had become the wife of the king of Portugal[139] did they finally have to give up hope.

MARRIAGE TO SIBYLLE OF JÜLICH-CLEVES

They very quickly returned to the old plan for a marriage with Sibylle. Counts Wilhelm von Nassau, Wilhelm von Neuenahr, and Philip of Solms took an interest in the matter and ensured that no other suitor had stolen a march on the Saxon prince.[140] In June 1525, they also asked Luther for advice. He advised concluding the matter, for it was not good to delay.[141] Unfortunately, the letter he wrote on this to Elector John was not preserved for us; he did not regard it as necessary to write to John Frederick, since the prince had stated

---

133 I cannot decide whether Sleidan's statement (p. 92b)—that Hannart said that they did not need to keep faith with heretics—is correct.

134 J. J. Müller, *Historie*; Lanz, *Korresp.*, 1:109.

135 Neudecker and Preller, 62.

136 That is, John Frederick.—Tr.

137 Förstemann 1:214f.; Lenz 1:113f. also agrees.

138 Wolf came on August 6 and remained until the nineteenth. Spalatin seems to have been concerned that he should not be treated too rudely (Spalatin ap. Menck, 2:636f., his August 17, 1524, letter to Warbeck; Schlegel, 211). Wolf was sent to the elector once again in December 1524, and on February 22, 1525, Spalatin ate with an embassy from Ferdinand (Förstemann 1:225, Spalatin's February 22, 1525, letter to Warbeck; Goth. Bibl. Cod. chart. B. 26, fol. 141). At that time, they could certainly not be dealing any longer with the marriage.

139 Kolde, 54f.

140 Reg. D. No. 58 I.

141 WA Br 3:525. I would understand this passage with Köstlin (1:732) and against Enders (5:190) as referring to the planned marriage.

that he would submit completely to the will of his father.[142] This, in fact, was the attitude of John Frederick. Just as with the engagement to Katharine, so here, he did not at all interfere but was at their disposal. However, some letters from 1527 and 1528 do clear up for us his personal feelings; he was not concerned about marrying but submitted to the wish of his father; at the same time, he hoped that through marriage, he would obtain a freer, more independent situation, and perhaps even his own household.[143]

The official marital negotiations began in April 1526 with talks between councilors from both sides in Bensberg.[144] The marriage, above all, had a political goal, and it now depended on settling the existing differences in a way satisfactory to both sides. They actually agreed <23> that in case the Jülich-Cleves dynasty died out, the united duchies would fall to the Ernestine line; in return, they needed to renounce their feudal claims on Jülich.

Now the "inspection" could proceed; the prince met with Sibylle and her mother on April 13 in Cologne. Above all, everything depended on whether or not he would be pleasing to Duchess Maria. That was the case; she was "pleased with the prince." It is hardly expected that the still not fourteen-year-old Sibylle would have made much impression on John Frederick. In a letter that he wrote to his father on April 19, he was rather lukewarm: "As Your Grace knows, I was in Cologne and found things such that I was pleasing and so much was undertaken in the matter that I regard it as settled." He added: "The councilors from both sides should get together and confer further on some supplementary matters."[145]

The articles dealt with here had called forth the greatest excitement among the councilors from Jülich-Cleves. John Frederick had given the best guarantees for his own person, but with reference to the Saxon feudal claims, he had to state that without Duke George, his father could undertake nothing in this matter, and that, therefore, he also could agree to nothing without his father. In the name of his father, he also wrote on May 13 from Torgau that they would seek what they had to claim only in amicable and legal ways, by which nothing else is said than that they would not renounce their claims. The councilors on the other side were of the opinion that with this, the advantages of the marriage were on the whole made illusory, and they advised the duchess to break

---

142 WA Br 3:525.

143 Cf. p. 38 <27>.

144 They are given in detail by Bouterwek, *Zeitschr. des Bergischen Geschichtsvereins*, Bd. 7:112f.; I essentially follow him.

145 Reg. D. 58 I, handwritten original.

off the negotiations; she, however, since they had come so far, did not want to turn back, and in June, submitted the matter to her diet.[146]

The negotiations were then taken up again on July 26 in Cologne and continued at the beginning of August in Mainz; but now no further yielding was to be obtained from Saxony. Without a Saxon renunciation, the marriage agreement was concluded on August 8 and signed on the ninth by the elector and his <24> son in Speyer.[147] The parents of the bride raised no objections. The most important stipulation of the agreement was that in case the Jülich-Cleves male line died out, John Frederick and Sibylle or their male descendants would retain the whole inheritance,[148] while Sibylle's other sisters should receive a settlement of money. The assent of the estates and ratification of the emperor would obtain greater stability for this agreement. John Frederick allowed his bride a "life annuity" of 5,600 gulden, while she brought him a dowry of 25,000 gulden. This was to be paid on the wedding day. But when there were difficulties about this, John Frederick renounced it in order not to delay the wedding. At the end of August, he had gone to his bride, and it appears to have been at his suggestion that the nuptials took place already on September 8 or 9 in Burg an der Wupper.[149] The young prince then stayed a few weeks with his parents-in-law, journeyed with them and his young wife to Stockheim to Count von Rabenstein, and on October 11, again arrived in Weimar.[150] He came alone, for even though they had hastened the wedding, bringing the bride home was postponed until all the negotiations about the conditions of succession, the assent of the estates, and the ratification of the emperor were completed. Much was still written back and forth about this; in January, John Frederick set off once more for the Rhineland.[151] He brought along a draft of the instructions for the embassy to the emperor,[152] but it was many years before they succeeded in getting the emperor to ratify the <25> agreement.[153] The negotiations with the estates were more favorable. After the electoral prince and his spouse had bound themselves to sign a declaration in which they pledged to observe the

---

146 Below 1:88f.

147 Spalatin ap. Menck, 2:660.

148 Dithmar, *Cod. diplom. zu Teschenmacher, Annales Cliviae,* No. CVI. On the contradiction between this stipulation and the simultaneous maintenance of the older Saxon claims, cf. Ritter, 7.

149 The circumstances are in Bouterwek, 116f.; Spalatin ap. Menck, 2:662, has September 8; according to a letter that John Frederick wrote to his father on September 11, 1526, it was the ninth (Reg. D. 58 I, handwritten original); perhaps this was John Frederick's mistake.

150 Spalatin ap. Menck, 2:662; September 11 letter of John Frederick.

151 Heß published the account of the journey in *Ztschr. f. thür. Gesch.*, N. F. 10:511f.

152 E.g., the copy in Loc. 10561.

153 In Innsbruck and Augsburg in 1530, lengthy negotiations took place because of this (Lanz, *Korresp.*, 1:394f.; Seckendorf 2:194; J. J. Müller, 673f.).

"privileges, customs, and rights" of the estates, they made no objections to recognizing the succession agreement. Things were concluded on March 17 in Jülich-Berg and on May 15 in Cleves-Mark.[154] John Frederick did not wait for this but returned home in the middle of March, after it was settled that the bringing home of the bride would take place on the Sunday before Pentecost (June 2).[155] The duchess then set out on May 7 to conduct her daughter to her spouse. Even if, against John Frederick's will, she traveled incognito and past Eisenach, he did everything he could so that the reception would turn out worthy of her, "without regard for cost."[156] He and his father met and welcomed the ladies just before Torgau. Then followed extensive festivities; numerous personages gathered together, tournaments were held, and even the old elector took part for the last time in his life.[157] The cost of bringing the bride home amounted to no less than 19,250 florins.[158]

After they had celebrated, the negotiations were again taken up. On June 9, the duchess handed over to the elector the dowry of 25,000 Rhinish golden gulden; on the tenth, she conveyed the silver plate; and on the twelfth, after the electoral prince and his wife had signed the declaration for the estates, all formalities were concluded.[159]

Whoever then looked at the gigantic John Frederick next to the slender Sibylle, who had scarcely outgrown childhood, could certainly think that here politics had joined together a truly unequal pair and would forecast nothing advantageous for the marriage. But those apprehensions were not fulfilled. <26> Instead, the two characters were excellently suited for each other. John Frederick and Sibylle, as far as we can judge, got along very well together, so that later Luther could point to the marriage of the Saxon prince as a model. Even the letters of Sibylle later to her husband in prison testify to a very affectionate relationship.[160]

Much contributed to the happy outcome of the marriage, so that the difference of faith still present in 1527 was soon set aside. As a bridegroom, John Frederick had never made a secret of his evangelical conviction; Myconius always accompanied him to the Rhineland and daily preached before him. On

154 Below 1:89–91.

155 *Am Sonntag vor Pfingsten (2. Juni)*; this does not seem correct. In 1527, Easter fell on March 27, which means Pentecost was May 15; June 2 was two weeks after Pentecost.—Tr.

156 May 21, 1527, letter from John Frederick to Anark von Wildenfels (Reg. A. 236, handwritten original).

157 The "old elector" is John the Steadfast.—Tr.

158 Reg. D. 58, II–V. Bb. 4342.

159 Dithmar, No. CVIII.

160 Published by Burkhardt in the *Ztschr. des bergischen Geschichtevereins*, vol. 5.

September 8, he had consecrated the couple, in spite of the fact that Sibylle had come to Torgau still as an adherent of the old faith. Soon, however, her husband succeeded in converting her, and in 1528, in Torgau, she went over to the Lutheran Church.[161] Her later letters, and especially her attitude toward Luther, show us that this was the deepest conviction of her heart. Her first letter to Luther was on January 14, 1529 (which we possess); it was written a few days after she delivered her first son, John Frederick the Middler, on January 8.[162] The letter shows us that she already then knew Luther personally; it also shows us the good relationship between the couple. We will later come back to this family relationship, but will now touch on just one point.

THE CONDUCT OF HIS OWN ROYAL HOUSEHOLD

When he decided to marry, John Frederick cherished the hope that now he would have his own separate household. He had so far been kept on a somewhat tight leash and hoped that now his own fixed income would be assigned to him. Before the wedding, he had told his father that he was <27> not very interested in marrying, but he wanted to obey his father; he asked then for "something of his own" from which he could have his livelihood. If this was not granted to him, then he would like to get something for himself from the dowry in Jülich or Cleves. The elector had the chancellor and von Wildenfels deal with him and finally stated that he would be kind to him; he and his wife would be maintained at the court in such a way that they would have no reason for complaint. New negotiations took place after the nuptials were completed, but the prince was again paid off in general assurances. When a new attempt a few days after the bride was brought home met with no better success, in the winter of 1527, he finally submitted a detailed memorandum.[163] He repeated his request "to establish his own way of life" and threatened that if this did not happen, he would have to go among the people—that is, borrow—because he did not receive enough from his father. John, whose support was fixed by the difficult financial situation of his states,[164] was not disturbed by this; he refuted each point of his son's memorandum and concluded with the statement that

---

161 Grulich, *Denkwürdigkeiten der . . . Residenz Torgau*, 43.

162 Enders 7:40. The difficulty of the dating is removed by the fact that John Frederick the Middler was actually born in Weimar, not in Torgau, according to which Beck, Pose, and Devrient are to be corrected (Reg. O. No. 156, fol. 68 and Loc. 9604, *de vita ducum Saxoniae*, fol. 9b.

163 Reg. D. 58 II without date. Official Document No. 5; see p. 101 <98>.

164 Cf. Burkhardt, *Landtagsakten*, introduction.

he had no reason to complain and with the request that he be satisfied.[165] Only after the electoral prince had repeated his wishes once again in a letter of July 14, 1528,[166] did he achieve a definite result: from the fall quarter[167] of 1528 on, his quarterly allowance was increased from 50 florins to 125 florins, and that of his wife from 75 florins to 100 florins.[168] However, John Frederick could not yet obtain a separate household and accounting. Until 1532, he, with his family, remained incorporated in the household of his father.[169] There seems to have been a change planned for July 1532. Because of the importance that was attached to the journey of the electoral princess and her sons at that time to Coburg,[170] <28> it seemed that there would be a real division of the household.[171] It was only a few weeks before the death of John when the desired independence was given to the electoral prince in full measure.

---

165 Reg. D. 58 V rough draft without date. Official Document No. 6; see p. 104 <101>.

166 Reg. D. 58 V, handwritten original. Official Document No. 7; see p. 104 <102>.

167 *vom Quatember cruc. exalt.*, that is, "from the quarter in which the festival of the elevation of the cross occurs," which is September 14.—Tr.

168 Reg. Bb. 4344.

169 Cf. Reg. Bb. 4352.

170 Cf. the July 5, 1532, letter from Hans von Minkwitz in Torgau to John Frederick (Reg. A. 247; Official Document No. 26; see p. 140 <140>).

171 This seems to be what Fabricius's comment (8:30) refers to: "The elector sent away his son . . . who would be living for some time at Coburg in France."

<29> Chapter 2

JOHN FREDERICK AND THE REFORMATION

FIRST TRACES OF RELIGIOUS FEELINGS

People like to look into the life of the child for traces of the later characteristics of the man. Several anecdotes have been handed down to us from the youth of John Frederick the Magnanimous that are supposed to prove he already then had the devout mind that later distinguished him. Unfortunately, all the anecdotes appear so late that we do not venture to make use of them. They agree very well with the character sketch of the prince. The surroundings in which he grew up were on the whole well suited to make him devout in the view of his time. His father and especially his uncle were men who zealously joined in the ecclesiastical practices of their time; no one was the equal of Frederick the Wise in venerating and gathering relics. Scarcely a day passed without listing an "offering" of both princes in the ledgers, and John Frederick followed their example insofar as he had the opportunity to do so. Whether a tradition that he was too devout even for his father[1] has any claim on credibility cannot be decided, but a December 24, 1519, letter from John would speak against this.[2]

The devout tendencies present in the prince were strengthened by his teachers. Spalatin and Colditz <30> were both theologians, and even though they were devoted to humanism, they certainly did not neglect the religious education of their pupil. This naturally stayed first on the usual paths. In the

---

1 There is an illustrated booklet that certainly comes from a later time, *Das ganze Leben und Historia des aller theuersten und werten Mannes Herzogen Johann Friedrichen,* where it says under the fourth picture:

> His father spoke to his son,
> You want to be too devout,
> Whoever tries to believe too soon
> Must suffer much in his life.

2 Cf. pp. 42 <30> and 99 <96>.

1519 inventory, we find listed, among other things, "a silver picture of Mary hanging from an Our Father, a gilded symbol of St. Anne," and the like. Among the books, we find the *Garden of the Soul*, a life of St. Bonaventure, and several passions and legends of the saints, since they were suited to serve as a basis for the traditional religious instruction. In addition—the most interesting part of the official documents—there were already numerous writings of Luther: the *Proceedings at Augsburg*,[3] the *Seven Penitential Psalms*,[4] the *Explanation of Psalm 110*,[5] *A Meditation on Christ's Passion*,[6] and *The Blessed Sacrament of the Holy and True Body of Christ and the Brotherhoods*.[7] We may conclude from this—unless we want to believe that this was at John Frederick's own initiative, since he had had the opportunity to hear Luther preach at Weimar in September 1518[8]—that Colditz was responsible for the fact that his pupil already as a youth was filled with the spirit of Luther.

FIRST CONNECTIONS TO THE REFORMATION

Actual proof for John Frederick's friendly attitude toward Luther comes first from the year 1520; when his father urged him on December 24, 1519, to go to the Sacrament,[9] we can just as easily conclude that he was religiously indifferent or very conscientious, as he had doubts called forth by the new teaching. Nonetheless, it is noteworthy that in March 1520, Luther already considered dedicating the *Treatise on Good Works* to the young prince.[10] Veit Warbeck zealously advocated Luther's teaching with the prince. The first direct reference to Luther we have is in October 1520.[11] <31> At that time, John Frederick wrote the reformer a letter (which unfortunately has not turned up) in which he assured him of his good will, revealed his great liking for Luther's doctrine, and

---

3 LW 31:253–92.

4 First edition in 1517 (WA 1:158–220); second edition in 1525 (LW 14:137–205).

5 WA 1:690–710.

6 LW 42:3–14.

7 LW 35:45–73.

8 Köstlin, *Luther*, 1:201.

9 Official Document No. 2; see p. 99 <96>.

10 March 25, 1520, letter from Luther to Spalatin (WA Br 2:75). LW 44:15–114.

11 I do not venture to cite the October 22 letter of Veit Warbeck.

Cyprian (*Nützliche Urkunden*, 1:454–57) has it directed to John Frederick, and others follow him; only Bolte (xxv–xxvii) considered John to be the one addressed. Since the letter, as Professor Ehwald very graciously informed me, has no address, this question is hard to decide. Some sentences of the letter sound somewhat pedantic, and John Frederick had in fact at that time also written to Frederick the Wise. Luther's letter on the thirtieth to John Frederick has much in common with Warbeck's letter. However, Eck sent the bull of excommunication to John, but hardly also to John Frederick.

informed him that he was also seeking to influence the elector in his favor.[12] He even sent Luther a copy of his letter to the elector.[13] Luther answered on October 30, confessed his fearlessness in spite of the bull, but expressed his apprehension that the University of Wittenberg would be harmed by Leipzig.[14] Now first he was inclined to dedicate a writing to the young lord, and he chose for that the exposition of Mary's song of praise, the Magnificat.[15] He was happy he could report to him on December 20, 1520, that he had received an answer to his writing to the elector[16] that was very favorable to Luther. In addition, in this letter, he again very decisively professed Luther's doctrine; he frankly called him his "spiritual father."[17] It cannot be asserted with certainty that this decisive attitude of the seventeen-year-old prince was brought about by his father.[18] In addition to Warbeck's influence, we can certainly assume influence from Spalatin. In a December 21, 1520, letter written from Coburg in his own hand, John Frederick thanks Spalatin for dedicating a booklet to him[19] and asserts at the end: "I will bear in mind your gracious request and cling to the Gospel."[20] When on January 16, 1521, Frederick the Wise instructed his brother to inform John Frederick that every day they were taking counsel against Dr. <32> Martin,[21] this is certainly to be regarded as proof that John Frederick could be counted on to defend Luther at court.

FURTHER CONNECTIONS TO LUTHER

The prince obviously made no secret of this friendly attitude toward Luther, even when he stayed in Worms in February, and Aleander was certainly well-informed when he reported to Rome on February 28 that "the nephew of the elector is much more heretical than his uncle, as all the world knows."[22] It was truly well-deserved when in the spring of 1521, Luther dedicated to the prince

12 The content of the letter comes from Luther's reply.

13 This fact comes from the prince's December 20 letter.

14 LW 48:181–83.

15 December 3, 1520, letter of Spalatin to Elector Frederick; Waltz, *Zeitschr. f. K.G.*, 2:121. LW 21:295–358.

16 The fact that John Frederick was at this time corresponding with the elector and not Prince John actually comes from Luther's statement in his January 16 letter to Spalatin (WA Br 2:248); Kolde (26), however, regards it as possible that Luther made a mistake here and points out that according to the accounts, John and his son were almost constantly together in the last months of 1520 (Reg. Bb. 5558).

17 WA Br 2:237.

18 Becker, *Kf. Johann v. Sachsen und seine Beziehungen zu Luther* (Leipzig, 1890), 8.

19 That is, his translation of Plutarch; see p. 29 <15>.

20 Goth. Bibl. Cod. chart. A 378, fol. 2; the letter is printed in Official Document No. 3; see p. 99 <97>.

21 Förstemann 1:5.

22 Kalkoff, *Depeschen Aleanders*, 106.

the translation and exposition of Mary's song of praise, at the same time as thanks for his letter of December 20. Although the writing was first done at the Wartburg, Luther already wrote his letter of dedication to the young prince on March 10. He made use of the opportunity to attach some admonitions regarding his future calling as a ruler: what other people do only brings benefit or harm to themselves or a few other people, but lords are in a position to be harmful or beneficial to many more, depending on how far they rule, and so on—principles that certainly were not without impression on the devout heart of the prince.[23] John Frederick's answer to this letter has not been preserved for us, but from Luther's next letter to him on March 31, it emerges that he had added some inquiries for Luther on the good works of Christ and His sleep. It had struck him that in the Gospels, it is mentioned only once that Christ slept [Luke 8:23]. Luther answered that this sufficed to prove the natural, true humanity of Christ in this point. With reference to Christ's works, he agreed with the prince that Christ constantly acted according to the Father's good pleasure, since He looks not at the works but at the will doing the works. John Frederick seems to have brought up the further question of whether on the cross Christ prayed all of Psalm 22. Luther answered that it does not matter whether he believes that or not, since nothing is said about this in Scripture.[24] John Frederick's letter <33> was an interesting proof of both the detailed theological and biblical studies he had then already become engrossed in and, at the same time, the sophistries he could get lost in.

With his answer, Luther sent to the prince the first sheets of the Magnificat, but further work on this was interrupted by his journey to Worms. John Frederick certainly followed the proceedings there with lively interest; Veit Warbeck's letters to his father kept him up-to-date.[25] Spalatin justly believed that the prince would be interested in the lampoon he sent him, "Dr. Martin Luther's Passion."[26] John Frederick's June 10, 1521, letter to Spalatin shows that he did not neglect to write to Luther after the proceedings in Worms,[27] but he obviously knew nothing about Luther's residence, and Luther preferred not to answer him instead of betraying where he was. We also have no reason to think that John Frederick was informed about Luther's residence in

---

23 LW 21:297–98.

24 WA Br 2:294.

25 Even though in all these letters in Reg. E, the address is damaged, for the time being, we must accept that they were directed to John and not to John Frederick. RTA 2:850n1 certainly stirs up doubts.

26 Letter of John Frederick to Spalatin (Cyprian 2:259; cf. Lenz, *Kritische Erörterungen zur Wartburgzeit*, 29n2; Schade, *Satiren und Pasquille*, 2:108f., which belongs in the summer; RTA 2:896).

27 Enders 3:171f. (Luther left Worms on April 26 and entered the Wartburg on May 4.—Tr.)

the Wartburg even when he stayed with his father in Eisenach from August 30 to September 6.[28] John made use of his encounter with Luther to get advice from him on a theological question through which the Weimar Franciscans[29] <34> were seeking to stir up scruples in him. From what we have previously learned about John Frederick's theological studies, we would certainly think that he would have zealously taken part in the discussions of these questions. The next positive evidence of his religious pursuits comes from March 1522. The proceedings that had taken place in Wittenberg during Luther's absence had stirred him up; he now turned to Luther and asked for information on the questions of the reception of the Sacrament under both kinds, the necessity of taking the Sacrament with the hands, and the eating of meat on fast days. He seems to have revealed a certain inclination to radical innovations, since in his answer, Luther thought he had to restrain him. With the marvelous freedom and toleration that still distinguished him at that time, he explained that these things were unessential: "We are not Christians because we receive the Sacrament, but because we believe and love." It would certainly be better to receive the Sacrament under both kinds, but for the time being, we must still make allowance for weak consciences.[30]

We know nothing about the effect this letter had on John Frederick. Another half year passes without our learning anything about his religious development. In September, at the suggestion of Lucas Cranach and Christian Döring, Luther forwarded to him through Spalatin a copy of his New Testament. The prince was present when Luther preached six sermons in Weimar on October 19, 24, 25, and 26,[31] in which he spoke among other things about the duties of the secular government.

---

28 Reg. Bb. 5560. That John went to Eisenach with a large retinue is at the same time new proof that to that point, he himself knew nothing about the residence of the reformer (cf. Luther's September 9 letter to Spalatin, LW 48:305–10). In no case do we have reason to suspect ulterior motives in his visit; this visit was not at all remarkable, since the prince went to Eisenach every year in August for a few days.

29 This is the way I explain the *grisaei pharisaei et hypocritae* with Enders (3:234) against Lenz (p. 45). This is hardly speaking about the court of Frederick the Wise; at this time, the connection between the two courts was slight. What kind of difficulties the Weimar Franciscans were making for the prince is shown by their petition (Cyprian 2:240–52); according to Luther's letter to Stein (WA Br 2:619), this belongs in 1522.

30 John Frederick's letter has not been preserved; its content is taken from Luther's March 18 answer (WA Br 2:477); cf. also Luther's March 24 letter to Spalatin (WA Br 2:480).

31 Köstlin 1:521; Reg. Bb. 5561.

AT THE CENTER OF A STRONGLY LUTHERAN CIRCLE IN WEIMAR

After this, John Frederick more and more became the center of a strictly Lutheran circle in Weimar. Even if he kept his distance from radical innovations, he did not refrain from actively spreading the new teaching. A Weimar Franciscan, the later Weimar court preacher Johannes Voyt reports how he was active. He would[32] <35> secretly provide the prince with Lutheran books, which he would then read in the cloister with Friedrich Mekum and others. Since most adherents of the Gospel had by then left the cloister, Prince John, his wife, and his son retained Voyt because they liked to listen to him preach. He was forbidden to preach by the provincial chapter in Weimar, and yet he still preached at the special desire of the prince on New Year's Day.[33] This sermon was printed in Zwickau at Michaelmas 1523, so it presumably took place on New Year's 1523. A provincial chapter had been held in Weimar in August 1521,[34] and the second wife of John had died on October 8, 1521. Thus, John Frederick's activity in propagating the Gospel in the Weimar Franciscan cloister must go back at least to 1521.

It is no surprise that all the adherents of the new teaching looked trustingly to the young prince and sought contact with him. Euricius Cordus praised him in a poem first published in 1522 as the protector of the purity of the Gospel.[35] In September 1523, Jonas begged Warbeck through Lang to be excused because he had not dedicated a booklet[36] that had just been published to John Frederick; this had not happened because of the invective contained in it, which was not suitable for such a devout and gentle prince, but at his next opportunity, he would keep the promise he made to Warbeck.[37] He actually did then in 1524 dedicate his exposition of Acts to the prince.[38] In that letter, Lang himself applied to the young prince and asked for a gray jacket, in order finally to comply with John Frederick's repeated demands that he would ask him for something.[39] In 1525, Melanchthon finally dedicated to the young prince his

---

32 There is an extra *durch* before the turn of the page that has been omitted.—Tr.

33 Rabi, *Historien der Martyrer*, vol. 2, book 2, chapter 7, Bl. 318a, b.

34 Kapp, *Kl. Nachlese*, 2:471f.

35 Krause, *Cordus*, 83; Cyprian 2:259.

36 That is, his writing against Faber (Kawerau, *Der Briefwechsel des J. Jonas*, 1:87f.).

37 September 19, 1523, letter from Lang to Warbeck (Goth. Bibl. Cod. chart. B. 26, 12–14; Oergel, 21).

38 Kawerau 1:91f.

39 That is, his September 19, 1523, letter to Warbeck. See chapter 1, note 84 above.

writing: *Solomon's Collected Thoughts on Hebrew Truth*[40] with a dedicatory letter in which he especially <36> emphasized the duty of princes to be concerned about the arts and the humanities.[41]

AGAINST THE ANABAPTISTS

John Frederick's support became especially valuable for Luther and his work when from 1523 on, the fanatical and Anabaptist movements gained ground. Even the preacher in Eisenach, Jakob Strauß, and the Weimar court preacher Wolfgang Stein fell under their influence. While Strauß campaigned especially against usury, Stein developed the theory that the Mosaic Law must again be established, because it is not proper for a Christian to obey the imperial laws. The influential comments of the court preacher made an impression on John. John Frederick and Chancellor Brück, who advocated common sense, were in a difficult position with the old lord; to him, they seemed to be opposed to the divine Word, and they finally had no other choice left than to appeal for Luther's support. Through Veit Warbeck, the prince in June 1524 had these questions submitted to him for a decision. On June 18, Luther answered in agreement with John Frederick and the chancellor, which then provided John the victory over both of the preachers. Luther, however, immediately made use of the opportunity offered to him, perhaps also induced by a question from the young prince, to state his views on the fanatics in general, and on Karlstadt and Müntzer in particular.

The prince's answer on June 24 reveals how firmly he relied on the Wittenberg theologians. Stein should himself go to Wittenberg and "sow his wild oats because of Moses' tribunal," and he would have liked to compel Strauß into a disputation with Luther and Melanchthon, but Strauß knew how to work successfully against this with Prince John. Finally, John Frederick also turned against the fanatics in his writing and lamented their number: "Unfortunately, there are all too many fanatics, as God knows, and they make too much work for us." He believed that no better means could be specified against this than that Luther should travel from one city to another in the principality and, like Paul, see "what kind of preachers the cities had provided the believers. I believe that you can do no <37> Christian work among us in Thuringia. The preachers who are not qualified are to be dismissed with the help of the government."[42] In this

40 *Salomonis sententiae versae ad hebraicam veritatem*.—Tr.

41 CR 1:774f.

42 June 18, 1524, letter from Luther to John Frederick (WA Br 3:305); June 24 letter from John Frederick to

way, the thought of a church visitation was put into words.[43]

John Frederick's suggestion was carried out on a small scale in August of that same year. On July 1 or 13, John and John Frederick heard one of Müntzer's sermons in Allstedt.[44] They had the sermon sent to Luther, who was thereby induced to write his *Letter to the Princes of Saxony Concerning the Rebellious Spirit*.[45] Besides this, they invited Müntzer to Weimar for a hearing. This took place on August 1, with the result that Müntzer voluntarily removed himself from the land.[46] Now, however, it seemed even more desirable to advance against the other center of the fanatical movement, that is, against Orlamünde, from which Kahla, Neustadt, and Jena had been infected. When in August Luther himself went to these cities, we can possibly regard this as an effect of John Frederick's suggestion. In the meantime, Stein had come to his senses and accompanied the reformer. The Weimar princes cannot have spoken to Luther before his journey, since they returned to Eisenach from a journey only on the twenty-third; however, on the return journey, John Frederick had reported on his experiences, the "tragedy of Orlamünde," and set forth to Luther and Brück that they had a right to remove Karlstadt from Orlamünde.[47] Furthermore, this matter seems to have been overseen chiefly by John Frederick. Luther spoke and wrote to him regarding how Karlstadt answered his September 11 request for a hearing and disputation.[48] Luther turned to him on September 22 on account of the new preacher in Orlamünde, Dr. Caspar Glatz, so that John Frederick would bring about the final removal of Karlstadt from Orlamünde.[49] <38> Glatz himself then complained to John Frederick in a letter perhaps belonging in 1525 about the difficulties he found in Orlamünde and asked him to take steps against the sectarians there.[50] There can be no doubt that John Frederick was regarded as the particular enemy of the fanatical movements; many even express the opinion that Weimar church policy was at that time essentially made by him. It was at his instigation that in the first months of 1525, an attempt at visitation in Eisenach was made by Jakob Strauß and

---

Luther (WA Br 3:309).

43 Burkhardt, *Gesch. der sächs. Kirchen- und Schulvisitationen*, 3.

44 Reg. Bb. 5563. The elector was not there. In the travel book, "both my gracious lords" means John and John Frederick. The elector is the "most gracious" lord. The princes were in Allstedt also on the first. Kolde (G.G.A. 1902, 763) overlooked that.

45 LW 40:45–59.

46 Cf. Köstlin 1:678.

47 September 13, 1524, letter from Luther to Spalatin (WA Br 3:345; cf. WA 15:328).

48 Luther to Stein (LW 49:83–84).

49 WA Br 3:353.

50 Goth. Bibl. Cod. chart. Bd. 26, fol. 104ff., between the letters from Luther to John Frederick on May 15 and 20, 1525.

Burkhardt Hund.[51] On March 24, 1525, the Weimar Franciscan Heinrich Pomponius objected to him in a remarkable letter that the monks were forbidden to preach.[52] Finally, even Philip of Hesse reported to him in March 1525 about his attempts to convert his father-in-law, George of Saxony.[53] When the count once again returned to these attempts in the summer of 1526, he corresponded above all with John Frederick.[54] Even if it would perhaps go too far to conclude from this that John completely left the regulation of all these ecclesiastical questions to his son, yet it can certainly be gathered from this that people then were convinced that the word of the prince had very great significance in these matters.

John Frederick understood well how to distinguish between the pure doctrine of Luther and its radical abuses. Therefore, there was no danger that he would be confused about the truth of the new doctrine because of the peasants' revolt. When in May 1525, he stayed in the camp before Mühlhausen with Elector John and Prince George, he resolutely maintained his Lutheran viewpoint. George got to hear many words from him that he had not heard before.[55] John Frederick was not for a moment in doubt about the <39> antievangelical character of the Dessau League, and he resolutely expressed that in a letter to Margrave Kasimir of Brandenburg.[56] So perhaps a certain part in the decisions of his father can be ascribed to him; in opposition to the caution Frederick the Wise always observed, he openly embraced the Gospel, without regard for whether anyone would be offended by that.[57] The enemies were in part to be sought among the acquaintances of the elector himself and among the Saxon nobility, but we cannot specify who was the target of the frequent complaints and allusions in Luther's letters.[58] Besides this, especially Prince George had to be greatly provoked by what his cousin[59] did; the opposition, which since the division of the two lines had continued in all kinds of territorial and legal differences, was greatly increased by their different relationships to Luther. This

---

51 Burkhardt, *Gesch. der sächs. Kirchen- und Schulvisitationen*, 3f.

52 Reg. N. No. 19. Cf. Official Document No. 4; see p. 100 <97>. Wette (*Histor. Nachricht*, 1:44f.) treats the March 19 prohibition of preaching.

53 At their meeting in Kreuzburg; cf. Friedensburg, *Vorgeschichte*, 40f. (Philip of Hesse married Christine of Saxony [1505–49] on December 11, 1523, the daughter of George, duke of Saxony.—Tr.)

54 I will soon return to these attempts at another place.

55 Seidemann in der *Zeitschr. für histor. Theol.*, N. F. 11:643f.; Friedensburg, *Vorgesch.*, 8; Rommel, *Philipp von Hessen*, 2:85.

56 v. d. Lith, 111f.

57 "Our princes openly confessed and followed the Gospel," September 29, 1525, letter from Luther to Stiefel (WA Br 3:584).

58 Cf. for example, LW 49:120–25, 143–47; WA Br 3:615, 634.

59 John the Steadfast was his first cousin, making John Frederick his first cousin once removed.—Tr.

situation was felt to be very burdensome on the Ernestine side, and it can be regarded as evidence of how secure the elector and his son were in their faith when in 1525 and 1526, they again and again returned to the thought of a religious colloquy between the theologians on both sides in order to set aside the chief hindrance to their union, the religious difference. George did not enter into those discussions. When an Electoral Saxon embassy once again proposed the matter to him in July 1526, he referred them to the diet.[60]

THE 1526 DIET OF SPEYER

While this diet was meeting, John Frederick always supported the Gospel at the court of his father. Through Warbeck on March 26, Spalatin turned to him to get John to refuse to retain the papistic ceremonies at the diet; tolerating these ceremonies could awaken doubt about the elector's fidelity to his convictions.[61] <40> Through him, Count Wilhelm of Henneberg secured a judgment from Luther on monastic vows.[62] Even Philip of Hesse asked him on June 17 to see to it that the attendants of the elector not discredit the Gospel through indecent behavior.[63] John Frederick gladly fulfilled all these wishes, for he neglected no opportunity to act in favor of Luther's doctrine. At Cologne, for example, he was accompanied by Myconius as preacher, and right after his return, he sent Lutheran books to Count Wilhelm von Neuenahr, with whom he had met in Cologne and in Dillenburg, "in order to make a good Christian out of him."[64]

At the diet itself, John Frederick seems not to have stood out; even though he had first initiated the visitation, he held himself back when on the basis of its decisions, the new Church was zealously organized in Saxony and Thuringia. It may be that his marriage and the journeys connected with it claimed enough of his time, but he did not neglect always to be accompanied by his preacher. He was certainly very interested in the disputation that Myconius arranged for February 19, 1527, with the Cologne monk Johannes Korbach.[65] In general, it is obviously because of the lack of material that we can produce only sparse testimonies from the next years about the electoral prince's religious and

60 According to scattered documents in the Ernst. Ges.-Arch. I will return to these discussions. Karstens's statements in *Zeitschr. f. Thür. Gesch.* N. F. 4 need to be supplemented.

61 Schlegel, 244.

62 WA Br 4:80.

63 Seckendorf 2:45f.; Friedensburg, *Speier*, 291f.

64 Meinardus 1.2:178f.

65 Myconius, 51f.; Seckendorf 2:91f.

ecclesiastical interests; what we do have still suffices to show that at this time, no change took place in him in this regard. So, for example, Luther found that he fully understood when in 1526, he complained about the way the greedy Saxon nobility were acting against the monasteries and their inhabitants.[66] Luther's April 1, 1528, letter to him shows that the prince was busy with the visitation.[67] Although John Frederick's conduct in the <41> Pack Affair will be better handled later, yet we can call attention here to the fact that in his letters to his father, he always stressed most decisively that he would not concede anything that went against God and his conscience.

THE 1529 DIET OF SPEYER

Our sources become more plentiful again in the spring of 1529. While the elector and most of his councilors stayed in Speyer, John Frederick was left behind in Weimar to attend to the government. In this way, he received the opportunity to deal with the most varied questions about ecclesiastical administration. He had to deal with the visitation,[68] with filling pastoral vacancies,[69] and with the punishment of Anabaptists.[70] In all difficult questions, he turned to Luther for advice. He already had to deal with a question that would later cause him much grief: he had to take a position on the reformation in Naumburg; he had on hand ideas about how to do this in the best way.[71]

Even while John Frederick was occupied with these questions of internal church policy, his glance wandered continually to Speyer, and he followed the proceedings there with the liveliest interest. The electoral prince cherished the fear that the question of electing Ferdinand to be the king of Rome would be negotiated there; he regarded it to be the chief problem of Saxon politics to prevent his election, for, according to the experiences they had so far had with him in his hereditary lands, the king of Bohemia and Hungary was <42> the highest and greatest enemy and persecutor of the divine Word. He called him

66 January 1, 1527, letter from Luther to Spalatin (WA Br 4:149).

67 StL 21a:1122.

68 March 12, 1529, letter from John Frederick to Luther and others (WA Br 5:36); to Kötteritzsch (Kawerau 1:124); to Elector John on March 21 (Reg. A. 241).

69 April 13 letter to Luther (WA Br 5:52); April 23 letter from Luther to John Frederick (WA Br 5:58).

70 March 21 letter to Luther and others (WA Br 5:42).

71 There is a note in Reg. H., 10. L. fol. 85/86 about what kind of advice in agreement with the divine Word the elector, prince, and embassy who agree with it should seek for Naumburg and the common state (draft in the handwriting of John Frederick). Naumburg should ask to be received into the League, commit itself to the preaching of the divine Word, etc., and hold to it as arranged in the electorate by the visitation. This is probably dated March 25 or April 3, although the advice does not seem to have been followed (cf. Hoffmann, 66f.; Schöppe, 345).

a bloodthirsty tyrant against soul and body. It seemed necessary to him just for religious reasons to do everything they could to oppose the election of Ferdinand. He thought they could even make use of the Turks against his election.[72]

John Frederick's desire that Electoral Saxony make use of the opportunity of the diet to oppose the election of Ferdinand came true to only a very limited extent, and he was not always satisfied with the attitude of his father and the councilors. He felt they did not keep him up-to-date enough, and he was in constant fear that they would not be firm and resolute enough in matters of faith.[73] He finally had to be persuaded that these were unfounded fears. John was not restrained either by the offense of Catholic practices or by the prevention of evangelical worship, and in that way achieved the best results. The electoral prince learned this with joy: "I have heard with an especially delighted heart that (God be praised!) there are still people at Speyer who heard the divine Word with a sympathetic heart! May God grant that the adherents of the divine Word would be more than those who hear a sermon in Your Grace's lodgings!"[74] John Frederick also completely agreed with the protest against the decisions of the diet: "I have heard with special joy that the Almighty God has been gracious to Your Grace and the other princes and estates, so that through the writing that was handed in, Your Grace and the others have openly and without any timidity confessed God and His divine Word before many, and so that Your Grace together with the others has declared that you will remain with it and not be led away from it by human works. May Almighty God preserve Your Grace together with the others in this faithfulness, so that you remain in it forever!"[75]

For John Frederick at that time, opposition to the old Church was obviously the chief opposition; however, during <43> the Diet of Speyer, he also had the opportunity to busy himself with the great division within the Protestant side. From Speyer, Minkwitz reported to him that a meeting of Luther and Melanchthon with Zwingli and Oecolampadius was being planned in Nuremberg. The electoral prince very much agreed with that. He had scarcely a doubt on which side the victory would be; since he simply regarded Zwingli and Oecolampadius to be the two rebels, he had already sufficiently given expression of his attitude toward them.[76] The prince does not seem at that time to have had a

---

72 Cf. pp. 74f. <69> and Official Document No. 8; see p. 105 <102>.

73 His letters on March 26 to Elector John; on April 4 to Anhalt; on March 23 to Minkwitz.

74 His letter on April 4 to the elector (Reg. E. fol. 37a No. 83, Bl. 76f. original).

75 His letter on April 26 to the elector (Reg. E. fol. 37a No. 83, Bl. 100; cf. Seckendorf 2:129; Jagemann, *Joh. D. Beständige* [Halle, 1756], 32).

76 March 30 letter from Minkwitz to John Frederick (Reg. E. fol. 37a, No. 83, Bl. 72f., original); April 12 letter

complete concept of the enormity of the opposition, since in his May 1529 plan for the league, he regarded the reception of the Swiss Confederation into the league to be very possible.[77]

THE DIET OF AUGSBURG

Nothing came of the plan for a religious colloquy in Nuremberg. When Philip of Hesse again took this up in a different form, Melanchthon applied on May 14, 1529, to the electoral prince to induce his father to forbid the Wittenberg theologians to participate in the planned religious colloquy. John Frederick readily granted this wish.[78] We know nothing about the attitude he then took toward the Marburg Colloquy, its preparations, and its results.[79] In February or March 1530, Luther dedicated to him his translation of the prophet Daniel; in the dedicatory letter, he praised John Frederick's desire and love for Holy Scripture and its wisdom; he further praised him because he had little love for controversy and doing harm; "those who like his princely conduct daily do the same."[80] From this, we can conclude that Luther had no reason to be dissatisfied with the behavior of the prince. I cannot say whether the opposition to Landgrave Philip into which John Frederick fell at the Diet of Augsburg had anything to do with the division in the Evangelical Church. <44> At all events, this diet offered the electoral prince the opportunity to demonstrate his evangelical convictions in various circumstances. When they took counsel at the electoral court about whether the elector should attend the diet at all, the electoral prince with Brück advocated the viewpoint that his attendance was definitely advisable, and his will carried through.[81] He then arrived in Augsburg on May 2 together with his father; indeed, he would not have hesitated to enter further into the den of lions and travel to Innsbruck to meet the emperor, if the elector would have permitted him to.[82] He trusted, to be sure, on the good relationships he had in the associates of the emperor; he even sent Lutheran books to the electoral ambassador Hans von Dolzig, such as Luther's *Exhortation to All Clergy Assembled at Augsburg*, which he could distribute to appropriate people.[83]

Not too much can be established about John Frederick's participation in

---

from John Frederick to Minkwitz (Reg. E. fol. 37a, No. 83, Bl. 222b–24, draft in his own handwriting).

77 Cf. p. 78 <73>.

78 CR 1:1064f., 1077f.

79 Cf. Lenz, *Briefwechsel Philipps*, 1:13.

80 WA DB 11/2:380–87; WA Br 5:1534.

81 Cf. J. J. Müller, 432f.

82 CR 2:48f.

83 June 10, 1530, letter to Dolzig (Förstemann, *U.*, 1:239–41); LW 34:3–61.

the deliberations after the arrival of the emperor in Augsburg. On June 16, he represented his father, who was not feeling well, when they gave the emperor their answer refusing to take part in the Corpus Christi procession.[84] John consulted him together with Brück and Melanchthon for advice on the imperial proposition.[85] During the negotiations that preceded the presentation of the Augsburg Confession, he seems not to have been in agreement with Melanchthon's extensive willingness to compromise. Melanchthon complained about him to Luther and asked him to write to the electoral prince that they should be somewhat more compromising toward the emperor.[86] Luther actually did compose a letter to the prince, but tore it up again, in order not to give him unnecessary worries.[87] The sincere letter that Luther then actually wrote on June 30 to John Frederick, however, leaves the influence of Melanchthon's demand unmistakable <45> when it says: "Of course the emperor has a devout heart and is worthy of all honor and virtue; too much honor cannot be given to him because of his person. . . . May Your Princely Grace have patience for the sake of God and the emperor!"[88]

Meanwhile, the Confession had already been presented, also with John Frederick's subscription. After the Catholic Confutation came out against it, a somewhat anxious time of waiting began. They had to be ready for the steps the emperor would take, and every rumor about that was easily believed.[89] Since on the Protestant side they did not desire a complete rupture, it is understandable that John Frederick returned home in high spirits after he heard on August 5 from one of the "great lords" that there was hope for an armistice.[90] In fact, the emperor resumed the negotiations in the form of deliberative committees. John Frederick was among the fourteen from the Protestant side who belonged to the second of these committees, and so had the opportunity to display his ready wit, Bible knowledge, and wide reading, for the anecdotes we possess have been handed down well enough that we can regard them as historical. Spalatin, who was present for part of the negotiations, said that the prince "conducted himself in a very Christian, stable, and good way."[91] In his funeral sermon for John Frederick, Menius put it this way: many who were

---

84 J. J. Müller, 527; Förstemann 1:270; Schirrmacher, 59f.

85 J. J. Müller, 568.

86 WA Br 5:386; Kolde, *Luther*, 2:592f.

87 June 29 letter from Luther to Melanchthon (LW 49:329).

88 WA Br 5:421.

89 Enders 8:275n2; Keim, *Schwäb. Reformationsgesch.*, 188–89 on the rumor spread by Pastor Schneid and its effects.

90 August 6 letter from Jonas to Luther (WA Br 5:533).

91 *Annales*, ed. Cyprian, 189.

present then at the colloquy were "conscious that His Electoral Grace spoke to the point, that the papistic sophists Eck and others were blushing with shame, and the learned on our side were delightfully amazed."

In particular, there are three stories that have come down to us, all three well attested. Once, the prince drew attention to a glaring contradiction between Eck and Cochläus, the two chief spokesmen for the opposition, in their statements about the <46> veneration of saints in the Old Testament.[92] Another time, when Eck was expounding a citation furnished by Cochläus from a writing of Luther on confession in which Luther spoke in a completely Catholic sense, Melanchthon did not know what to answer, but the electoral prince said, "Yes, he wrote that some ten or twelve years ago."[93] When in their discussion about granting the cup, Eck applied the words "Drink of it, all of you" (Matthew 26 [:27]) only to the clergy, since "all" means the same as "priests," John Frederick immediately interjected that then the words "You are clean, but not every one of you" [John 13:10] must also mean "You are pure and devout, but not the priests and clerics"![94]

These discussions also did not lead to a resolution, and after the discussions of a select committee of six people also failed, staying at the diet no longer had any purpose. The princes began to leave; the elector also wanted to go but was again and again detained by the emperor. For John Frederick, there was no longer any reason to remain. There was scarcely any prospect of success in the discussions that still took place privately and into which John Frederick was once again drawn when Heinrich of Brunswick proposed to him and Brück in a private meeting at night that the properties of the monasteries should be placed into the hands of the emperor until a general council was held.[95] When the counter proposal of the Protestants that the property should be confiscated and managed for two years by honest noblemen was turned down by the emperor, John Frederick had already started the journey home. He traveled past Coburg, where he met with Luther on September 14. As a sign of his devotion, he presented him with a signet-ring, which he had had made during the diet,[96] and invited him to travel home with him. Luther, however, preferred to wait for the elector and his retinue.[97] <47> The electoral prince cheerfully

---

92 This is attested above all in *Dr. Martin Luther's Warning to His Dear German People*, 1531 (LW 47:46).

93 Reported by Cochläus himself in "Herzog Georgs Entschuldigung wider Luthers Verantwortung," 1533, Bl. 12; Ernst Salomon Cyprian, *Historia der Augspurgischen Confession* (Gotha, 1730), 200–1.

94 Luther's Table Talk (Erl. 61:394).

95 Hortleder 2:242; J. J. Müller, 857–62.

96 Enders 8:27f., 30, 87.

97 September 15, 1530, letter from Luther to Melanchthon (WA Br 5:621f.).

reported to his father on the fifteenth that Luther was fresh, healthy, and happy and had grown such a large beard that people could scarcely recognize him. He also thought, however, that he could not let this opportunity pass without exhorting the elector to steadfastness in matters concerning the divine Word.[98]

John Frederick wrote down his own final thoughts on the course of the Diet of Augsburg and especially on the conduct of the Evangelicals there in a letter to Duchess Elisabeth of Saxony on October 8[99] and in a letter to Count Wilhelm von Nassau on October 24.[100] In the first letter, he chiefly addressed the question of the monastery property and most dogmatically denied that the negotiations failed; in the second letter, he explained that they had compromised as far as possible and now must entrust the future to God, for they would rather have an ungracious emperor than an ungracious God.

In fact, in the months after the Diet of Augsburg, an important change took place in the views prevailing at the Electoral Saxon court, since they became convinced of the necessity and validity of opposing the emperor.[101] On the other hand, because of his May 1529 memorandum, it seems doubtful to me that it can be asserted that John Frederick now first overcame his aversion to cooperation with the South Germans.

In the next period, it was primarily political concerns that claimed the prince's attention; his chief principle remained that you can only do what you can justify before God and your conscience; our task here will be to determine what the electoral prince's opinions were. While there are scarcely any statements from which we can gather anything about the prince's relation to the Zwinglians,[102] a sharp <48> opposition to the Roman Church continued. For example, when he was in Cologne in December 1530 to protest the election of Ferdinand, he was not induced even by the emperor's well-expressed desire to suspend evangelical preaching or to refrain from eating meat on fast days.[103] Even the harsh treatment the emperor is supposed to have given him, according to a Roman report, scarcely made an impression on him.[104] Over against the proposals of the counts of Dessau and Neuenahr in August 1531, he stood

---

98 Förstemann, *U.*, 2:450f.

99 Reg. A. 241, draft in his own handwriting; Official Document No. 20; see p. 133 <132>.

100 Reg. E. fol. 37a. No. 88, draft in his own handwriting; Official Document No. 21; see p. 136 <135>.

101 Winckelmann, 36.

102 When in Smalcald in 1531, the question of admitting the Swiss Confederation to the league came up, he said that he must first inform his father (Winckelmann, 294). I have not been able to establish whether he had any part in the harsh instructions that Minkwitz and Dolzig received for the Diet of Frankfurt (Torgau, May 24; Reg. H., 52, No. 8, fol. 52f.; Winckelmann, 123).

103 Spalatin ap. Menck, 2:1121.

104 G. Heine, *Cartas al emperador Carlos V.*, 100f.

firmly with the Augsburg Confession; in Schweinfurt in April 1532, he was delighted with the success Spalatin's preaching had,[105] and Spalatin gave his full praise to the religious attitude of the prince.[106]

THE NEGOTIATIONS FOR PEACE; JOHN FREDERICK AND LUTHER

However, his evangelical convictions did not prevent John Frederick from making significant concessions for the achieving of peace. For this, he could count on the full approval of the reformer. These peace negotiations lead us, after all, to the question of how great Luther's influence was on John Frederick at this time; was his opinion authoritative for the electoral prince in every matter? It deserves to be stressed that he was not at all afraid to express his deviating viewpoint at times most decisively. For example, he was very dissatisfied with the dispute that broke out in 1529 between Luther and Prince George in connection with the Pack Affair;[107] he labeled the writings of both as libels and was surprised that they had reached as far as the Rhine to the count of Neuenahr, since they seemed to him to be of no great value.[108] In a letter to Dolzig, <49> he once expressed his dissatisfaction that all letters had first to be sent to Wittenberg before a decision was made; thus everything naturally happened slowly.[109] During the peace negotiations, it was his opinion that Luther's compliance was somewhat too great.

To be sure, when John Frederick did after all go to Schweinfurt and then defended this step to the count and others, he could be certain of Luther's approval; on the other hand, it was not at all his opinion that because of the love of peace, they must yield on the question of the election, as Luther advised.[110] Likewise, during the deliberations in Schweinfurt, the electoral prince seems to have had the viewpoint that they could not yield further than they had done in the proposals they had made to the mediators, and that, above all, they dare not abandon all future adherents of the evangelical doctrine.[111] For all that,

---

105 April 1 letter to John (Reg. H., 63, No. 16, vol. 1, fol. 105f., original; Seckendorf 3:20).

106 Verpoortennius, *Sacra analecta*, 68f.

107 See p. 68 <61>.

108 March 13, 1529, letter to Neuenahr (Reg. E. fol. 37a, No. 83, Bl. 210–12, draft in his own handwriting; Official Document No. 9; see p. 112 <110>); cf. also the April 12 letter to John (Reg. E. fol. 37a, No. 83, Bl. 225), and on April 14 to Countess Elisabeth (Reg. A. 240; Official Document No. 13; see p. 119 <117>).

109 Förstemann, *U.*, 2:735f.

110 WA Br 6:1773.

111 April 24 letter from John Frederick to John (Reg. H., 63, No. 16, vol. 3, fol. 31–36); May 4 letter to Neuenahr (Cornelius, 10:137; cf. Winckelmann, 187–209).

John Frederick himself then brought it about that, after nothing definite had been decided on this question in Schweinfurt, immediately after his return, John summoned Luther, Melanchthon, and other Wittenberg theologians to a consultation on the peace proposals at Torgau.[112] This conference took place already on May 13, and the numerous opinions of theologians we possess certainly belong at this time.[113] The theologians all took the viewpoint that they must be content with the peace if the emperor would leave the present confessors of the Gospel alone. The elector agreed with this viewpoint.[114] John Frederick, who also stayed in Wittenberg for two days, was in a very jovial mood and spoke with the theologians for hours.[115] Like Brück, he did not completely agree with their advice. Perhaps it was he and the chancellor who prevented taking the <50> theologians along for further peace negotiations in Nuremberg.[116] The Saxon representatives seem to have based their statements there on Luther's opinion, but they were certainly not all that surprised to find little approval for this. The opinions that were brought along from the other side were completely opposed; the view was "that what Dr. Luther and the other scholars at Wittenberg permitted in their advice and reflection cannot be granted or accepted before God and conscience." Yet they hoped to come to a compromise.[117] In reality, the unity of the Protestants was preserved since they simply adhered to their Schweinfurt resolutions without regard for those in Wittenberg. John Frederick and Brück seem not to have been completely at ease with this, and on June 21, the electoral prince asked his father to send the copies they had of the Nuremberg discussions to Luther and the other Wittenberg scholars, and to ask again for their opinion, so that he could act according to it.[118] John readily granted this wish.[119] The result, however, did not at all conform to John Frederick's hopes. The deliberation that Luther and Jonas submitted, which the elector could forward to his son already on June 30 with a declaration of his fullest agreement, was even more compromising than the earlier one.[120] The theologians advised complying with all the demands from the emperor, and that went too far even for the most yielding of the Protestant estates. Although

---

112 May 7 letter to John (Reg. H., 63, No. 16, vol. 3, fol. 109, original; Official Document No. 24; see p. 139 <139>).

113 WA Br 6:307f., 313f.; Burkhardt, 205.

114 May 26 letter from John at Torgau to Count Philip (Reg. H., 70, No. 19, copy).

115 May 20 letter from Melanchthon to Jonas (CR 2:590f.).

116 CR 2:591.

117 June 9 letter from John Frederick in Nuremberg to John (Reg. H., 65, No. 17, vol. 1, fol. 16, 21).

118 Reg. H., 65, No. 17, vol. 2, fol. 42–44. Official Document No. 25; see p. 140 <139>.

119 Burkhardt, 205f.

120 LW 50:56–60. June 30 letter from John to John Frederick (Reg. H., 65, No. 17, vol. 3, fol. 2/3).

Luther had written on June 29 directly to John Frederick a letter filled with earnest admonitions to peace,[121] he made no secret of his divergent viewpoint. On July 9, he wrote to his father that "no ambassador either of the margrave or from Nuremberg, no matter how lenient they were on this matter, <51> could regard this article as acceptable without offense to divine glory."[122] On the same day, Brück said that Luther would certainly have a different viewpoint if he knew all the facts.[123]

We cannot properly say that the Protestants later again departed from this precisely expressed viewpoint, so that Luther's view finally triumphed,[124] for in the meantime, the negotiations assumed an entirely different character. They no longer negotiated about an actual agreement but about an armistice, a public peace,[125] and for this, new proposals arrived from the emperor, which the mediators submitted to the Protestants on July 4. Luther's desires may have been effective to the extent that they decided not to put any great difficulties in the way of accepting the new imperial proposals, in spite of Hessian opposition. The articles were returned with a few amendments coming in part from John Frederick himself,[126] but they decided ahead of time not to let peace be wrecked by these demands.[127] The elector completely approved of this viewpoint,[128] and on this basis, then, the peace was concluded. John Frederick thought he could be satisfied with what had been achieved; at all events, he had acted most conscientiously[129] and assisted in achieving a goal that would not be completely without benefit for the Reformation.

---

121 WA Br 6:332.

122 Reg. 65, No. 17, vol. 3, fol. 58–60. Official Document No. 27; see p. 142 <141>. Cf. Seckendorf 3:22; Winckelmann, 233, 236.

123 Reg. H. 65, No. 17, vol. 3, fol. 65.

124 Winckelmann, 236.

125 Cf. the letter from John Frederick to Neuenahr (Cornelius 10:149f.; Ranke 3:296n).

126 Reg. H., 65, No. 16, vol. 4, fol. 111, a copy of the elector's draft from July 4 with John Frederick's amendments in his own handwriting; cf. Seckendorf 3:21.

127 July 9 letter from John Frederick to John, as quoted in the previous paragraph.

128 July 14 letter to John Frederick (Reg. H., 65, No. 17, vol. 3, fol. 78–79).

129 His view is expressed very plainly in the July 28 letter to Neuenahr (Cornelius 10:149f.).

<52> Chapter 3

POLITICAL ACTIVITY UP TO THE NUREMBERG STANDSTILL

INTRODUCTION TO POLITICS

John Frederick's first introduction to the world of politics took place when on April 29, 1520, the Saxon and Hessian princes met in Nordhausen to renew their fraternal inheritance. This resulted in a very interesting and, in part, animated debate, but it cannot be reported that John Frederick participated in it at all. That was certainly not to be expected. Here, however, he did have the opportunity to get to know his young cousins John of Saxony[1] and Philip of Hesse and make friends with them; moreover, they were admitted into the fraternal inheritance.[2] He then entered into a wider circle when he arrived with his father in Worms on February 8, 1521, and on the tenth, both had an audience with Charles V.[3] John Frederick could then still be considered his brother-in-law.[4] The reason for the presence of the two princes, apart from John's general duty to participate in the diets, was the desire to pursue a fief from the emperor and to deal with the claims of the Wettins to Jülich. However, it would have been too expensive if they had awaited the completion of these things; so both princes again left Worms already on February 23,[5] since John left his brother full power of attorney to represent him in these questions.[6] Nothing at all is said in this power of attorney about the marriage question, but we can certainly <53> suspect that this question was one of the reasons for the journey of John and his son to Worms.

1 The son of George, duke of Saxony, John (1498–1537) married Elisabeth of Hesse on May 20, 1516.—Tr.

2 Reg. D. 495; J. S. Müller, *Annalen*, 73.

3 RTA 2:787.

4 Because of the arrangement for John Frederick to marry Charles's sister Katharine.—Tr.

5 RTA 2:804, 808.

6 February 21. RTA 2:808.

PARTICIPATION IN ADMINISTERING THE LAND

This is how John Frederick was introduced to the large world of politics. It was more important, however, for him to learn the way government worked in the regions he would one day rule. We can speak very specifically about when the impetus was given for this, for on March 25, 1521, Frederick the Wise expressed to his brother the wish that, since he was no longer as capable as before and the councilors accomplished too little, John himself could see to it and could "train his son for the business" to see how he would do. He is now old enough and can look after his own affairs.[7] For all that, I cannot furnish any proof that John took into account his brother's wish. In general, for many years, there are only very insignificant traces of any participation of John Frederick in the government of the Ernestine states. He took part in the diets of 1523 and 1525,[8] but without standing out in any way; he occasionally acted as a judge in 1525,[9] and in the instructions for the journey to Friedewald, John granted him full authority to receive and decide the petitions of his subjects.[10] He did think about administrative concerns; this is shown by his memorandum of May 1529, in which he recommended that according to the pattern of ducal Saxony, also the Ernestine regions should be divided into a series of jurisdictions.[11] Especially from 1530 on, he took a lively interest in the discussions at the diet; he himself conducted some of the negotiations with the estates.[12] Important questions like finance reform were submitted to him for his judgment,[13] and even when he was out of the country, <54> he attentively followed the business of the diets, as his letters to John show.[14]

PARTICIPATION IN NEGOTIATING WITH THE ALBERTINES

The relationship to the Albertines always had the closest connection to questions of internal Electoral Saxon politics. I cannot say how far John Frederick

7 Förstemann 1:13.

8 Burkhardt, *Landtagsakten*, 1:153, and Reg. Bb. 5564.

9 Loc. 8233, fol. 142b, 146b, Loc. 8786; Faselius, 8.

10 Reg. H., 2, B.

11 Reg. H., 10, L. fol. 81–84; see Official Document No. 17; see p. 128 <126>.

12 Burkhardt, *Landtagsakten*, 1:239, 243, 256–62.

13 Burkhardt, *Landtagsakten*, 1:196, 218, 220.

14 January 6, 1531, letter to John from Hambach (Loc. 10671 "Schreiben und Bedenken," fol. 166–67); March 28, 1531, letter from Weimar (Reg. H., 59, No. 13, fol. 207); April 5 from Georgenthal (ibid., fol. 25f.); June 25, 1532, from Nuremberg (Reg. H., 65, No. 17, vol. 2, fol. 53–56), etc.

was in the know about these extraordinarily complicated controversies, but some of his letters show that, in spite of all the indignation at the conduct of Prince George,[15] he was again and again ready to offer the hand of peace. He fully agreed that there should constantly be "consultations" among the councilors to attempt to bring about a settlement; when in 1529, Wolf von Schönberg suggested that he should himself be the mediator, he was very ready for that.[16] A meeting between him and George's son John was planned, at which they could confer on the ways and means suitable for reconciling their fathers. I cannot establish that this took place; there is not a trace of John Frederick's participation in the Grimma Decree, which at least brought a certain settlement of the differences.

John Frederick seems to have been more interested in politics at large than in local administration and strife with neighbors. Hans von der Planitz thought that he was ready in 1522 to represent his uncle on the imperial council in Nuremberg, but Frederick himself was doubtful about that.[17] The political activity of John Frederick was for some years still limited to his father taking him along to various meetings of princes[18] <55> and presenting him at various courts.[19] An opportunity for independent activity came up first in 1525.

It was Prince Philip who gave his cousin the occasion to earn his political spurs. Already in March, he had invited him to a meeting in Kreuzburg; but since he had written that it was all right with him if Prince John came along, he participated in the conference. We do not know for sure which questions of a political nature were discussed there along with the religious questions, but there is a definite probability that they were busied with commotions among the peasantry.[20] During the Peasant War, John Frederick seems to have been given no opportunity for independent action; we find him constantly in the

---

15 This comes out especially in the April 14, 1529, and October 8, 1530, letters to Duchess Elisabeth; see Official Documents Nos. 13 and 20; see pp. 119 <117> and 133 <132>.

16 December 18, 1529, letter from John Frederick at Torgau to Wolf von Schönberg (Reg. A. 242, clean copy; Official Document No. 19; see p. 132 <131>).

17 Planitz, *Berichte*, 164, 176, 181.

18 There was a meeting in Naumburg in October 1522 of both Saxon lines, the elector of Brandenburg, and the princes of Anhalt (Spalatin ap. Menck, 2:616; Reg. Bb. 5561); in Jüterbog in October 1523 with the elector of Brandenburg, King Christian of Denmark, and other princes (Spalatin ap. Menck, 2:631; Enders 4:258; Reg. Bb. 5562; cf. also Spalatin, 2:633, 635f.).

19 In January 1525, in Ilmenau and Arnstadt; in January and February, in Berlin and Stettin (Reg. Bb. 5564).

20 On the Kreuzburg meeting, see Seckendorf 2:35f.; Friedensburg, *Vorgeschichte*, 40/41; Stoy, 26; Seidemann in the *Zeitschr. f. hist. Theol.*, N. F. 13 [1849], 175f.; Friedensburg in *N. A. f. s. Gesch.*, 6:118f. John Frederick mentioned in his April 4 letter to the count (Reg. N., 39, fol. 4) that he was forwarding to him a writing on the tithe, from which I conclude that they had discussed this question. Reference to the Dessau Alliance of July 1525 is naturally excluded (Enders 5:147).

company of his father,[21] who became the new elector at this time, and whose two campaigns he took part in.[22] Like John, he seems to have been filled with a conciliatory and kind attitude toward the peasants.[23] It was also only in the entourage of his father that John Frederick took part in the meeting on August 6–8, 1525, with Margrave Casimir and George of Brandenburg in Saalfeld,[24] and likewise on August 11–13 at the meeting with Prince George in Naumburg.[25]

FRIEDEWALD

<56> Then on October 5, Landgrave Philip sent his treasurer, Rudolf von Waiblingen, to John and suggested to him joint action at the diet summoned for St. Martin's Day at Augsburg and common defense against all the dangers threatening the area of religion.[26] When John said he agreed completely with this,[27] the landgrave further asked him to send his son to him at his hunting lodge Friedewald with the goal of greater agreement. The elector consented,[28] and on November 1, John Frederick, accompanied by Hans von Minkwitz, set off from Torgau past Leipzig, Naumburg, Weimar, Gotha, and Eisenach to Friedewald.[29] There they discussed the preparations for the diet. A second point of discussion was the things that concerned the divine Word and the Holy Gospel. Philip had held a meeting at the end of October in Alzey with the electors of the Palatinate and Trier; John Frederick received instructions from his father to inquire what the landgrave had learned about their attitude toward the religious question.

The meeting at Friedewald was further connected to the princes' alliance suggested by Prince George before Mühlhausen for mutual support against the revolt of their subjects. John and Philip undertook at this time to recruit new members for this league. They became convinced very quickly that Prince George was seeking to give an antievangelical character to the league; in spite of that, they continued their efforts, and so laid the basis for a league of evangelical-minded princes. John Frederick was to report to the landgrave which

---

21 Reg. Bb. 5564.

22 Reg. Bb. 5564 and Spalatin ap. Menck, 2:1113; Struve 3:103; Fabricius 8:26f.

23 This is shown by Mühlpfort's letter to Roth (Kolde, *Analecta Lutherana*, 64f.), and the July 8 letter from John Frederick to Katharine of Saxony (Seidemann, *Schenk*, 120f.).

24 Friedensburg, *Vorgesch.*, 11; Schornbaum, 73f.; Reg. Bb. 5564.

25 Friedensburg, 18f.; Reg. Bb. 5564.

26 Friedensburg, 41f.; Rommel, *Urkb.*, 10f.

27 Friedensburg, 43; Ranke 6:125f.

28 October 30 letter from John to Philip (Friedensburg, *Speier*, 63n).

29 Reg. Bb. 5564.

princes, counts, and cities the elector hoped to win, not to mention furnishing information on the status of the negotiations with Prince George. For a further discussion of these matters, he was to suggest a meeting between the elector and the landgrave. In the proposals he laid before the electoral prince in Friedewald, the landgrave was more resolute than the elector in emphasizing <57> the idea of a union of the Evangelicals. He also hoped to win the electors of the Palatinate and Trier for this, already thought about the reception of the most important South German cities, and proposed a meeting of those princes and cities who agreed after Christmas.[30] John Frederick seems to have completely agreed with the views of the landgrave, and in Torgau, they approved of the Friedewald agreements without hesitation.[31]

With this, however, the content of these discussions has not yet been exhausted. There were points they discussed with each other only orally,[32] and we have reason to think that these dealt especially with the question of the election of the Roman king. Already in 1524, King Ferdinand had his eye on this goal and planned to win Saxony through the marriage of John Frederick with Katharine.[33] In the fall of 1525, reports again reached Elector John about these plans; he corresponded about this with Count Philip, and through him with Elector Ludwig of the Palatinate, and proposed a meeting between him and Ludwig for this purpose.[34] Since this letter had to have come already in October, it is very probable that John Frederick had spoken with Philip about this matter in Friedewald. The brisk correspondence between <58> Ludwig of the Palatinate, Philip, and John that took place in the next months touched again and again on the question of the election, partially in veiled hints, partially in separate letters. John Frederick had a not insignificant part in this,[35] and, as we will see, he did not afterward lose sight of the question of the election of Ferdinand as Roman king.

In general, the Friedewald meeting was particularly well suited to inform

30 Cf. Ranke 2:171; Friedensburg, *Vorgeschichte*, 46f.; *Speier*, 110f., 114; Baumgarten 2:548f.; Stoy, 31f. The instruction for John Frederick is in Reg. H., 2, B, and incompletely printed in Ranke 6:126. John Frederick's record of the discussions is in Ranke 6:126f.; cf. Friedensburg, *Vorgesch.*, 48f. I am not entering into some points here that are unimportant for us; cf. Friedensburg, *Vorgesch.*, 120f.; *Speier*, 80n1.

31 November 21 letter from John to Philip (Reg. H., 2, B, draft; Friedensburg, *Vorgesch.*, 58f.).

32 In the November 21, 1525, letter to Philip, John speaks about an oral report from his son (Reg. H., 2, Lit. B, draft; Friedensburg, *Vorgesch.*, 58f.). That this dealt with the matter of the election is shown by a November 26 letter from John Frederick at Torgau to Philip (Loc. 10671 "Schreiben und Bedenken" fol. 16f., draft in his own handwriting).

33 Friedensburg, *Speier*, 21.

34 This comes from Ludwig's November 3, 1525, letter to Philip (Loc. 10671 "Schreiben und Bedenken," fol. 13, copy; Friedensburg, *Speier*, 116n1).

35 Some of the notes are certainly dealing with the question of the election (Loc. 10671 "Schreiben und Bedenken," Reg. H., 2, B; Friedensburg, *Speier*, 117f.).

him about the most important questions in the politics of his time. The material we have is not sufficient to warrant the assertion that he pursued the idea of an evangelical league with the same interest he had in the question of the election. He did not at all stand out in the discussions that preceded the Gotha-Torgau League; he was only present at the Magdeburg conference. He only again received the opportunity for participation in politics through his personal affairs, that is, through his engagement with Sibylle. When the negotiations about the marriage ended so very favorably for Saxony so that no rights had to be given up, this was above all thanks to the electoral prince.[36]

JOURNEYS INTO THE RHINELAND

John Frederick's repeated journeys into the Rhineland gave him the opportunity for all kinds of connections that surely contributed much to the widening of his horizons. It had been the counts of Nassau, Neuenahr, and Solms who mediated the union with Sibylle. He had probably met them already in April 1526 in Cologne. He then accompanied Wilhelm von Nassau to the Orange Castle Dillenburg. He formed a long-standing friendship with him as well as with Wilhelm von Neuenahr, a friendship to which we are indebted for many interesting letters, and which began in these days when he was looking for a bride. This connection was of great value for the prince, especially because of the close connection of both counts to the imperial court.

<59> But it would scarcely have been possible at that time to spend time with Wilhelm von Nassau without learning about the great dispute in which he and his brother Heinrich were entangled with Landgrave Philip of Hesse; for many years, they disputed about the possession of the county of Katzenellenbogen. In fact, with the support of the duchess of Jülich, the landgrave asked the Saxon electoral prince to take charge of the negotiations on this matter. When John Frederick visited the landgrave on his journey home, he had the opportunity to report on these proposals. Philip had no objections to Saxon mediation and pointed to the approaching diet as a suitable time, a proposal that John Frederick delivered to Count Wilhelm and which met with his approval. The landgrave was later prevented from visiting the diet; however, negotiations did take place there under the mediation of the elector of Saxony and his son, without, of course, achieving peace.[37] This dispute over the Katzenellenbogen inheritance is occasionally mentioned in the correspondence

36 Bouterwek, 113f.

37 Meinardus 1.2:175f., 178f.

of John Frederick in the next years; it was certainly no easy task for him to remain impartial and not offend either one when he was closely connected with both.[38]

A concern that got his attention every time John Frederick stayed in the Rhineland was the almost constant recruiting.[39] When now in September 1526, John reported to him about armaments and recruiting in Lower Saxony, this greatly disturbed him. He was of the opinion that, provided they were not allocated for the banished king of Denmark or against Albrecht of Prussia, they could only be designed against Anhalt or <60> Electoral Saxony; therefore, they must take countermeasures and above all keep their eyes on Wittenberg.[40]

MEETINGS WITH LANDGRAVE PHILIP

Of the political activities of the Protestants in 1526, that which seems to have especially interested John Frederick was the planned embassy to Spain. Mention is made of this in almost all of his letters; in January 1527, he was commissioned to negotiate with the landgrave about this.[41] We can generally assume that at the frequent meetings with him, for which John Frederick's journeys to the Rhine gave him opportunity, all the important political questions of the day were thoroughly discussed. There probably was no lack even then of differences of opinion between the two young princes. For example, when Heinrich of Brunswick journeyed to Spain in the spring of 1526, John Frederick was filled with the deepest suspicion of him. Philip, however, was still at that time friends with Heinrich and asked the electoral prince not to be prejudiced against him.[42] Another time, John Frederick was endeavoring to get Albrecht of Prussia accepted into the evangelical league but found little inclination in the landgrave for this.[43] Then again, the electoral prince may have shown little sympathy for Philip's desire to get Saxony to aid Ulrich of Württemberg; we have no statement from him on this question; at all events, he had nothing against it when Philip brought the banished Württembergers to

38 On October 15, 1531, Wilhelm von Nassau advised him "as much as possible to stay away from the courageous young man's affairs," in order not to incur the displeasure of the influential count of Nassau (Reg. H., 50, No. 5, fol. 96).

39 April 19, 1526, letter from John Frederick at Dillenburg to John (Reg. D. No. 58 I, handwritten).

40 September 22, 1526, letter from John Frederick at Hambach to John (Reg. H. 3. C, fol. 44–47, handwritten).

41 May 16, 1526, letter from John Frederick at Torgau to Wilhelm von Nassau (Meinardus 1.2:178f.); September 11 to John (Reg. D. No. 58, I); January 31, 1527, to John (Reg. D. No. 58, II).

42 April 19 letter from John Frederick to John (Reg. D. No. 58, I); June 6, 1526, letter from Philip to John Frederick (Reg. N. 50, handwritten).

43 "I think the league is so full, it will become too heavy," January 31, 1527, letter to John (Reg. N. 50).

his farewell party. Although the negotiations were zealously carried out there, nothing is known about John Frederick's participation in them.[44]

THE PACK AFFAIR

<61> On this occasion, there were some statements made on the Catholic side[45] that caused such suspicion and nervousness among the Protestants that in the following year, they fell victim to the Pack deception.[46] John Frederick had a very prominent part in the discussions brought about by that. He first became involved with the matter when in Eisenach on February 5–7, he attended his father's discussions with the landgrave,[47] and then at the end of the month journeyed to Kassel on behalf of the elector to make inquiries with Philip, probably about his accomplishments in Dresden.[48] However, the landgrave and his councilors had no desire to speak openly with him about that, but instead prevailed on him to invite his father to a meeting with the count in Weimar. John Frederick fulfilled this wish; at the same time, he dispatched Dolzig to Torgau to report to the elector on everything that had happened in Kassel. He himself traveled directly to Weimar.[49] There the meeting took place on March 9 between John and Philip that led to a fairly aggressive league to oppose the alleged Catholic alliance. In the participation of John Frederick in these discussions, we receive the insight that the landgrave and John at that time agreed on a modification of the Hessian-Saxon fraternal inheritance; we have a copy of this from his own hand.[50] Perhaps we should assume that this discussion was so confidential that only the electoral prince knew about it and served as secretary. On the other hand, there is no trace that John Frederick had any part in the discussions conducted on the Saxon side in March and April to gain more members for the Weimar League.[51]

<62> Only occasionally do we find him occupied with the Saxon

---

44 Cf. Stoy, 189f.; Wille, 29f.

45 Schwarz, 12.

46 In 1528, Otto von Pack, an official of Duke George of Saxony, turned over a copy of a document to Philip of Hesse. This document was intended to provoke the estates that supported the Reformation to war against the Papists, for it described an alliance of the most powerful propapal sovereigns of the empire for the purpose of stamping out the Lutheran heresy. The document was eventually found to be bogus, but not before much harm was done.—Tr.

47 Reg. Bb. 5567.

48 Philip must then have returned home from Dresden, from where he had departed on February 18; on the twentieth, he was in Altenburg (Bb. 4344).

49 All of this is according to the February 27, 1528, letter from John Frederick in Kassel to John (Reg. H. fol. 22. D, handwritten).

50 I intend to give the details elsewhere.

51 Schwarz, 47–50.

mobilization.[52] Besides that, he gave attention from Torgau to the proceedings in the regions of the enemy, especially in Brandenburg and Brunswick, and reported to the landgrave all the suspicious symptoms.[53] The landgrave gladly made use of the opportunity this gave him to affirm his willingness to furnish help, but on the other hand to ask the electoral prince to be active in favor of the common cause with his father.[54] In spite of this, under the influence of the advice of his theologians, a certain disenchantment had come over the elector. We cannot establish how much John Frederick was influenced by this, since we do not possess his letters to Philip during April.[55] Because of sickness, John Frederick did not take part in the second Weimar meeting from April 28 to May 2.[56] It brought about a softening of the March 9 agreements since they resolved, before attacking the enemy, to request the bishops of Würzburg and Bamberg and the archbishop of Mainz to commit themselves to peace and to a "guarantee" of peace.[57] Scarcely had the elector and the count separated, however, when two things happened that seemed to entail a complete change in the situation. Count Hoyer of Mansfeld came to Weimar on behalf of King Ferdinand to warn him about the intrigues of Landgrave Philip.[58] Besides, he now learned that <63> Philip had offered his mediation to the imperial government.[59] Supported by the reports of the elector of Mainz to the landgrave,[60] all of this seemed to raise the prospect of peace, and his theologians would have strengthened him in the view that he could let no such opportunity pass. So perhaps on May 10,[61] he dispatched his son, accompanied by Anark of Wildenfels, to the landgrave. He was to express to the count the elector's desire not to send a message to the bishops but for now only to send an embassy to the government to move them to take steps in keeping with their offer to send ambassadors to the bishops to induce them to peace and to the guarantee of peace. They must first await the answer of the government and of King Ferdinand to

52 Burkhardt, *Landtagsakten*, 1:187f. No. 353, 354.

53 This comes from Philip's April 23 letter to him (Reg. H. fol. 22. D, original).

54 Already on March 27, he wrote to him: "Support the cause; your life and that of your father depends on it as much as my life. I hope to fight, as you well know" (Reg. H. fol. 22, D, handwritten original with a postscript). On April 23, he again promised to do his best for the original plan: "If this had been followed in Weimar, it would now be over" (Reg. H. fol. 22, D; cf. Ranke 3:31n).

55 According to a gracious note from the archives administration, they are not present in Marburg either.

56 Burkhardt, *Zeitschr. f. kirchl. Wissensch.*, 3:591.

57 Seckendorf 2:95; Schwarz, 56; there will be details on the Weimar agreement elsewhere soon.

58 Instruction for John Frederick, about May 10 (Reg. H. fol. 24. E. 24f., 112f.; Ehses, 52).

59 In the instruction, there is mention of the government's solicitation of the landgrave. This is something different from the mandate that called forth doubts in de Wette (3:332f.).

60 Schwarz, 62.

61 Already on May 11, there is a letter from John to his son (Reg. H. fol. 24. E).

the Electoral Saxon embassy to him, before they take further steps, in order not to be in the wrong. Only if the government took sides would they have the right to proceed on their own authority. The efforts of the Magdeburg councilors for peace in Electoral Mainz also awakened hopes for the best. Soon in Torgau people were almost certain that peace would be maintained. In spite of this, the electoral prince received the permission possibly to consent to send an embassy to the government and the bishops at the same time.[62]

The prince acted exactly in keeping with these directions. After he arrived in Kassel on the morning of May 16, he explained the instructions of his father on the same day to the landgrave in the presence of Ludwig of Boyneburg, Tyle Wolff, Friedrich Trott, and other Hessian councilors. Philip then pointed out the difficulties it would cause him to maintain his troops so long and also appealed to the Weimar agreements. Nothing else remained, then, for the electoral prince but to state that his father <64> would adhere to this and would approve of giving full authority to the councilors to be sent to Bamberg and Würzburg; yet at the same time, a written communication and inquiry would be sent to the imperial government.[63]

It would lead too far afield if we were here and now to follow the Kassel negotiations in all their details by means of the numerous letters of John Frederick. If we only keep our eye on the main point, then there is no doubt that there must have been some reason that the prince was in a warlike mood. This seems to be hinted at in the letter that Luther and Melanchthon directed to him on May 18.[64] The July 15, 1528, letter from Melanchthon to Camerarius shows this.[65] This comes finally from the warnings the elector directed at him during his stay in Kassel. We do not know the basis for these views; while he was in Kassel, as Melanchthon correctly observes,[66] John Frederick gave no reason for complaint. He and Wildenfels were completely correct and somewhat insulted in rejecting those fears; the electoral prince even asked once that the chancellor be sent to him so he could straighten everything out.[67] At all events, he occasionally took a different view of current politics than did the Electoral Saxon government; for example, he repeatedly asked most urgently for the Saxon draft of the writing they planned to send to the emperor, so that

---

62 All of this according to the instructions to John Frederick.

63 May 17 letter from John Frederick to John (Reg. H. fol. 24. E. Bl. 15, 16, 19).

64 LW 49:195–96.

65 CR 1:987: "Our prince and, shockingly, also his son greatly shrink back from war."

66 CR 1:987; cf. also 9:662.

67 Cf. the May 22 letter from John Frederick to John (Reg. H. fol. 24. E. Bl. 107–10); letter from Wildenfels to John (Reg. H. fol. 24. E. Bl. 88f.).

he could use it to restrain the landgrave from going public with his own draft, which John Frederick thought was very absurd. He did not receive it, because in Saxony, they were afraid that it would be published as a joint draft, which they did not want now; he finally could no longer restrain the landgrave from publishing his own. John also did not at first approve of the electoral prince accompanying Philip to Smalcald, because he feared that he would finally be drawn into the campaign. <65> John Frederick, however, explained that it was not because of arrogance that he went there; he was not as eager for war as they might think, but rather far from it.[68] We will venture to believe that he thought he was serving the cause of peace in this way, and John also finally gave his consent to it. They dared not spoil things with the count as long as they were not fully sure of peace. The preparations for war, which play a not insignificant role in the letters of John Frederick, also could not well be discontinued before they were sure of peace.

Even if the inclination to peace was not actually as strong in the electoral prince as it was in his father, and even if he here and there yielded too much to the landgrave, he was probably the most appropriate person to conduct these complicated negotiations, for Philip seems to have been in something less than a rosy state of mind. Already on the eighteenth, John Frederick was close to breaking off the negotiations.[69] He wrote on the twentieth that the landgrave was as hard to deal with as a dog on a leash who sees the quarry.[70] Anark of Wildenfels even stated on the twenty-second that any wild animal was easier to tame than he was.[71] It was certainly to the credit of John Frederick and his attendant that in spite of all this, they persevered with Philip, and they may have had a moderating effect on him. As already mentioned, they did not succeed in preventing him from sending an embassy to the bishops. Just as little were they able to prevent the landgrave from informing his provincial diet about the Catholic alliance, writing about this to Duke George,[72] and publishing this in the empire. However, they were concerned that, in spite of unpleasant delays, he waited for the answer of the bishops.[73] They pacified him on the question of the costs of his <66> mobilization by holding out the prospect that Saxony

---

68 May 23 letter to John (Reg. H. fol. 24. E. Bl. 102–4).

69 Letter to John (Reg. H. fol. 22/23 D. Bl. 54/55).

70 Reg. H. fol. 24 E. Bl. 29f.

71 Reg. H. fol. 24 E. Bl. 88f.; cf. Schwarz, 66.

72 Reg. H. fol. 24 E. Bl. 79; there is a second letter written by John Frederick on May 20.

73 The cause of this delay was that the Saxon councilors, who were supposed to wait for their instructions in Römhild, returned home without permission. May 18 letter from John Frederick to John.

would cover half of the costs.[74] When the answer of the bishops was not completely satisfactory, since they still had no answer from the government, the mood in Kassel again became very warlike. Even the electoral prince thought that they could demand a guarantee of peace from the bishops.[75] Meanwhile, however, they became convinced in Torgau that the bishops were guiltless in this matter. The elector began to fear that, after all, the Catholic alliance did not exist,[76] and desired to profit as much as possible from the matter: "Since His Grace did not see the original, as His Grace pointed out in Weimar, we were in truth frightened. Now His Grace wants to have many copies,[77] since he thinks that only in this way will the affair become obvious. If there is no further information about the alliance, then little will be accomplished."[78] Actually, in the meantime, in response to <67> his writing, the count received so many angry statements from the enemy and so many offers of mediation that he could no longer adhere to his plans for war but had to offer peace. John Frederick was also present at the peace negotiations that began on May 31 in Smalcald, but no details are known about his conduct there. He also seems not to have taken part in the polemical correspondence that was attached to the Pack Affair. Only occasionally did he speak about his own conduct there, above all in an April 14, 1529, letter to Duchess Elisabeth. Among other things, he rejected the accusation that it was his fault the landgrave adhered so much to Pack. Philip had not spoken with him about the matter for a long time, but only the last time he was present in Weimar; anyone could know what he advised him, since it was nothing dishonest but only what the landgrave could answer with honor and justice. He then turned indignantly to the assertion that he had misled the

---

74 In his instructions, John Frederick had been commanded to negotiate with the landgrave on this point. This was furiously debated on the eighteenth; finally, the electoral prince sent his father the landgrave's demand that Saxony cover half the costs, if they were not to become enemies over the payment. The elector was ready for that, but ordered his son to make precise inquiries about the actual expenditures of the landgrave. The prince promised to do this, but withheld from Philip any information about this in order first to await the decision of the bishops. On May 31, there was a meeting in Breitungen of Saxon and Hessian councilors at which Saxony said it was ready to cover half the costs if they did not reach an agreement with the bishops (Reg. H. fol. 24 F). Naturally, it was now a smaller sacrifice for Saxony to renounce its claim for restitution of costs from the bishops (Schwarz, 165f.).

75 May 24 letter from John Frederick to John (Reg. H. fol. 22 E. Bl. 131f.).

76 There was a letter from Prince George (dated May 21; cf. Schwarz, 85) and some secretive letters—I have not been able to determine who wrote them—that awakened this suspicion in the elector. Cf. his May 20 letter from Eisenberg to John Frederick, and his May 23 and 25 letters from Weimar (Reg. H. fol. 24, E. Bl. 63–66, 120–24, 139–40).

77 By the agency of the electoral prince, the landgrave was sent copies of the Dessau Alliance, the imperial instruction for Heinrich of Brunswick, the letter of the emperor to the counts of Nassau and Königstein, and the like. May 23 letter of the electoral prince from Rotenburg (Reg. H. fol. 24, E. Bl. 128f.).

78 From John's May 25 letter.

landgrave; he never advised him anything dishonorable.[79]

After the settlement of the Pack Affair, a somewhat more quiet time began for the young prince, although there seemed to be a large problem before him in the fall of 1528. Already in February 1527, the idea arose to send him to King Ferdinand to receive a fief.[80] The plan solidified in September 1528. All the participants for the journey had already been determined. Agricola would accompany them as preacher.[81] They had, indeed, already set off and reached Altenburg. There the whole procession turned around,[82] because the report from the councilors sent ahead to Prague about Ferdinand's conditions was not satisfactory.

JOHN FREDERICK AS THE REPRESENTATIVE OF HIS FATHER IN THE SPRING OF 1529

Then in the spring of 1529, John Frederick was given the opportunity for an extraordinarily brisk political activity. When the elector traveled with his councilors to the Diet of Speyer, <68> John Frederick was left behind in Weimar to rule the country. Dangerous times seemed to make that necessary.[83] Wildenfels and four other councilors were appointed to support him.[84] It appears from some letters of the electoral prince that he did not completely agree with being left behind and regarded his presence in Speyer as more necessary.[85] We are indebted to his being left behind for an extraordinarily large number of handwritten letters and opinions that apprise us not only about his frankly astonishing industry, but also about his political views in the most varied fields.[86] We have already observed the interest with which he followed the discussions on religious matters and have assembled the traces of his administrative activities. The question that occupied him most of all, however, seems to have been the question of the election of the Roman king. It had not been laid to rest since 1525.[87] I have before me a secret opinion of Albrecht von Mansfeld

79 Reg. A. 240; Official Document No. 13; see p. 119 <117>. I have so far not been able to locate John Frederick's 1537 writing to Neuenahr, as it is cited by Seckendorf 2:99.

80 Stoy, 191n1.

81 WA Br 4:562.

82 Reg. O. No. 24, fol. 133; Reg. D. 436.

83 March 13, 1529, letter from John Frederick to Neuenahr (Reg. E. vol. 37a, No. 83, draft; Official Document No. 9; see p. 112 <110>).

84 According to a list of the councilors who went along to Speyer and of those who remained behind (Reg. E. vol. 37a, No. 83, Bl. 19–21).

85 E.g., his April 4 letter to Anhalt.

86 These documents are mostly in Reg. E. fol. 371, No. 83 and Loc. 10671 "Schreiben und Bedenken."

87 Cf. e.g., Stoy, 135, 185, 211, 232f., 255.

to the elector dated March 6, 1527, in which he explains that the election of the "Antichrist" Ferdinand, which would lead to the crown being hereditary in the house of Austria, must at all events be prevented. They must make use of the opposition of Bavaria and establish relations with the electors of the Palatinate, Cologne, and Trier. If the emperor allows a free election, there is perhaps hope that they can elect a Christian king and that "the Roman Empire can be restored from the hands of the princes of Austria, who by birth are not worthy of this honor, to the princes."[88]

DELIBERATIONS ON THE CHOICE OF A KING

There was again greater activity in these matters as a result of the negotiations of the prior of Waldkirch, Balthasar Merkle, who toured Germany in 1528 on behalf of the emperor.[89] Among other things, he was commanded to work for the election of Ferdinand <69> as Roman king.[90] In June, he met with the Saxon elector in Smalcald, and then he seems once again to have been in Weimar in October.[91] His efforts stirred up much suspicion in John Frederick; they awakened in him the conjecture that this matter would above all be pushed at the Diet of Speyer; when in February 1529 the final preparations for attendance at the diet were made, he wrote down his views on the election of the king in a detailed "Reflection."[92] In some points, it is reminiscent of the 1527 opinion of Albrecht von Mansfeld. It was also John Frederick's opinion that the election of Ferdinand should not be allowed (1) because in that way, they would have a hereditary emperor, and (2) because of his hostile attitude toward the Evangelicals. People have not yet had to suffer under his hostility, but if he is elected, he would be made into the government to which according to Holy Scripture we must be subject. The only possible way of guarding against this, therefore, is preventing his election. This was not really to the advantage of the emperor, for then the empire would either have two heads, or he would have to leave the government of the empire to his brother and then only be king of Spain. In addition, he set forth the dangers of a double election and all its dangerous consequences; the party in opposition could easily get the

---

88 Loc. 10671, March 6, 1527, Allstedt, handwritten.

89 Cf. Ranke 3:81; Baumgarten 3:23.

90 Ney, 15.

91 At least on October 2/3, he was in Jena (Reg. Bb. 4344, 5568).

92 Loc. 10671 "The Election of King Ferdinand" concerning 1531, handwritten draft and copy; Loc. 10671 "Schreiben und Bedenken," copy. Here I provide only the main points and for the rest refer to Official Document No. 8; see p. 105 <102>.

idea of calling up the "common man," or joining up with England, France, or even the Turks.

In case the emperor should persist in his intentions, the electoral prince thought that Saxony must proceed in this way: It must first seek to win over the other electors so that they could jointly give a refusal to the imperial orator and in general only act uniformly in this matter; eventually they should send a message to the emperor to remind him of the Golden Bull and of his capitulation in the election.[93] If all or part of the electors were not in favor of this, then Saxony must turn to some friendly princes <70> and induce the princes to make overtures to the electors and remind them in turn of the stipulations of the Golden Bull. The princes must state their willingness to support the electors if any danger should come from their opposition. Eventually they could draw in the cities. John Frederick hoped that in this way, it would perhaps be possible to prevent the election of Ferdinand.

During the elector's stay in Weimar, John Frederick no longer had the opportunity to present his somewhat revolutionary views to him, so he had his reflections copied down and forwarded them to him in Gotha; at the same time, he asked him to talk the matter over with the prince of Anhalt and his councilors.[94] John seems to have been somewhat skeptical toward this matter; he questioned whether the princes John Frederick named "had the mind-set" he assumed they had.[95] Nevertheless, he promised to do his best. He actually then presented the reflections in Frankfurt to the prince of Anhalt, Hans von Minkwitz, Ludwig von Boyneburg, both chancellors Brück and Beier, and Melanchthon for their perusal and deliberation, and for his part, praised the industry of the electoral prince.[96] However, when John then arrived in Speyer and noticed that there was no talk at all about the election of the king and that no one spoke with him about the matter, he thought that for his part, he should not refer to it.[97] That, however, was not the view of the electoral prince! He set forth with good reasons that they naturally must first deal with Electoral Saxony; Saxony must take the lead if all the other electors are to be won over. What Waldkirch had accomplished was sufficient reason to begin negotiations with the electors; they should begin first with the Palatinate and Trier, and Wilhelm von Neuenahr can explore the situation with Cologne. If they could

93 The Golden Bull of 1356 established, among other things, that elections were to be handled by the seven electors of the Roman Empire, not by the Roman emperor.—Tr.

94 February 26 letter to John (Loc. 10671, "Concerning the Election of King Ferdinand," 1531, original).

95 February 27 letter to John Frederick from Gotha (Reg. E. Bl. 40, original).

96 March 14 letter to John Frederick from Speyer (Reg. E. Bl. 47, original).

97 March 30 letter to John Frederick from Speyer (Reg. E. Bl. 74, handwritten).

win these three, then the matter is already won; if this is not to be, then they must of course pursue the other ways developed earlier.[98]

John Frederick already suspected that his father <71> would not let his peace be disturbed by these arguments; he feared that they would delay too long, in other words, that they would sit down at the table and fall asleep over their food.[99] He did not trust the chancellors either.[100] Obviously, he could then have washed his hands in innocence,[101] but when he himself could do nothing, he regarded it to be his duty at least to work through his friends at the diet. Hans von Minkwitz, Albrecht von Mansfeld, and Wilhelm von Neuenahr must take up the matter. In fact, negotiations then took place with the elector of Trier and with the Cologne councilors, and this even resulted in discussions between the two spiritual electors and John. Both of them were not completely unapproachable and were little in favor of the election of Ferdinand. On the other hand, the elector of the Palatinate "did not know Saxon," and they could not really count on Mainz.[102] Further activity of the kind the electoral prince had developed in his memorandum seems not to have taken place, since they scarcely had any prospect of success. These statements of John Frederick are interesting for us, since they show how thoroughly he was involved with these questions and what bold ideas he had. In comparison with the slowness of John, at this time, he gives us the impression of an extraordinary alertness and liveliness.

OTHER POLITICAL ACTIVITIES AT THIS TIME

The election of the Roman king was certainly not the only great political question on which he sought from Weimar to gain influence. His friends in Speyer had to be active for him in various other connections. Thus on March 22, Minkwitz received a long memorandum forwarded to him for his negotiations with the prior of Waldkirch.[103] During his stay in Weimar, he had informed the electoral prince about the negotiations Prince Heinrich of Brunswick had

98 April 8 letter to John (Reg. E. Bl. 228–30, handwritten; Official Document No. 11; see p. 116 <113>).

99 April 12 letter to Minkwitz (Reg. E. Bl. 222b–24, draft in his own hand).

100 March 22 letter to Minkwitz (Reg. E. fol. 63–65, handwritten; Official Document No. 10; see p. 114 <112>).

101 April 12 letter to Minkwitz (Reg. E. fol. 63–65).

102 April 13 handwritten letter from Minkwitz to John Frederick (Reg. E. Bl. 87); April 14 letter from Mansfeld to John Frederick (Reg. E, Bl. 89–92, original; Official Document No. 14; see p. 122 <120>). We can doubt the honesty of the electors of Cologne and Trier, based on the statements they made already in 1526; cf. Friedensburg, *Speier*, 143n2.

103 Reg. H., 6, E, draft in his own hand and two copies.

carried out in Spain in 1526.[104] Among other things, <72> he had confirmed John Frederick's hunch that the prince reported to the emperor that the Evangelicals wanted to spread their teaching with force. When now Heinrich decisively denied this, even though it was clearly so in the emperor's instruction to him and from the imperial letter to the counts of Nassau and Königstein,[105] John Frederick desired further explanations from the prior, even if possible a kind of confrontation between Waldkirch and Brunswick in Speyer. It is clear from the further correspondence of the electoral prince with Minkwitz that Waldkirch now acted quite ambiguously and would not speak plainly, so that John Frederick finally had the negotiations broken off. This shows us that his opposition to Heinrich of Brunswick already had its roots at this time; moreover, a certain inclination to obstinacy was becoming evident in them.

Other than religious matters, the part of the discussions at the diet that interested John Frederick most was the question of aid against the Turks. It was his opinion that also this demand of the emperor came through King Ferdinand; he wondered whether they could not make use of the danger from the Turks to obtain compromises in the matter of religion, since a prerequisite for aid against the Turks was peace and justice in the empire.[106] He finally sent "some articles" on this question to the prince of Anhalt, Count Mansfeld, and Minkwitz.[107]

From the remaining content of the letters of the electoral prince from this time, it can perhaps be mentioned that the report of the death of the wife of Count Wilhelm von Nassau at once gave him the idea of Wilhelm marrying his oldest sister, Maria.[108] He did not again lose sight of this plan, which seemed to be advantageous for the house of Saxony, for the Evangelical Church, and finally for the settlement of the "Hessian Affair," until Count Wilhelm von Neuenahr informed him in <73> October 1531 that his uncle had married someone else.[109]

---

104 Cf. p. 67 <60>.

105 Both on March 23, 1526 (copies in Reg. 6, E; cf. Friedensburg, *Speier*, 84n2).

106 March 26 letter to John (Reg. E. fol. 37a, No. 83, Bl. 69/70, handwritten; Official Document No. 11; see p. 116 <113>).

107 April 4 letters to these three; April 8 letter to John, Official Document No. 12; see p. 117 <114>; April 12 letter to Minkwitz (Reg. E, op. cit., Bl. 221–24, 229). I have not been able to locate the "articles."

108 Maria (1515–83) eventually married Duke Philip I of Pomerania-Wolgast on February 27, 1536.—Tr.

109 April 4 letter to John, with an April 4 P.S. to Anhalt (Reg. E. op. cit., Bl. 76f., 243f.); list of what is to be spoken about with Count Philip of Solms (Reg. E. op. cit., Bl. 231f.); September 29, 1531, letter to Neuenahr (Reg. H., 50, No. 5, fol. 89f.; Official Document No. 23; see p. 138 <137>); October 15, 1531, letter from Neuenahr to John Frederick (Reg. H., 50, No. 5, fol. 91–93).

COLLABORATION ON THE LEAGUE OF THE EVANGELICALS

The Diet of Speyer had ended with a protest from the Evangelical estates against decisions by the majority in matters of faith, with a pronounced division of the empire. John Frederick completely agreed with this; however, it was also clear to him that the Protestants must now again take up their efforts at a league with redoubled zeal to be on guard against a "rash attack" from the enemy. He who was always eager to write had some "Reflections" ready. Ranke is certainly correct to put the undated "Reflections on Union for the Sake of the Gospel" of the electoral prince in May 1529.[110] The interesting thing in this opinion of John Frederick is that even though he was convinced of the validity of opposition to the other estates, since they could not be considered as powers ruling over the equal Protestant estates, he did not at all think of the emperor. It is further to be noted that he desired and thought it would easily be possible to include the South German cities and the Swiss Confederation; in the articles on the arrangement of the league, there seems to crop up a certain opposition to Count Philip in John Frederick's warning against choosing a too "impetuous" prince as leader. He obviously had the most interest in the military side of the question; he held forth in detail about this, and he also drew the consequences such a league would have to have for the individual estates when he dealt in a second document with the military measures that would become necessary for Saxony.[111] His proposals are carefully thought out and show that he regarded many of the Saxon administrative arrangements as in need of improvement. It also appears to me from these two opinions of the electoral prince that the difficulties Electoral Saxony made at that time in the politics of the league had their origin more in <74> Elector John than in his son.[112] On the other hand, in the negotiations that were carried on at that time between the Saxons and the Hapsburgs, about which we know nothing definite,[113] John Frederick seems to have been not entirely uninvolved; at least we have from him an instruction for Christoph Groß to Heinrich of Nassau with declarations of loyalty to the emperor, which seems to belong at this time.[114] As long as we know nothing

---

110 Ranke 3:117; Reg. H., 10. L. fol. 75f.; Official Document No. 16; see p. 124 <122>.

111 Reg. H., 10. L. fol. 81–84, draft in his own hand; Official Document No. 17; see p. 128 <126>.

112 It should be mentioned that John Frederick's demands reappear in the instruction for the Saxon councilors at Schwabach, but that the religious stipulations for reception into the league cropped up there anew (J. J. Müller, 281f.; cf. also Kolde, *Beiträgen zur Reformationsgesch.*, 98f.).

113 Lenz, *Zwingli*, 250; Baumgarten 3:16, 21f.

114 Reg. E. fol. 37a, No. 83, Bl. 233f.; the dating comes from the beginning of a July 8, 1529, letter from

specific about these negotiations, we can assume that they dealt with receiving the Saxon fief, which still had not been settled, and the ratification of the marriage of John Frederick. In spite of that, a journey of the electoral prince to Prague was planned in August 1529.[115] Further, his intention to participate in war on the Turks could have caused discussion. According to Spalatin's report, in the fall of 1529, he was to march at the head of several thousand men against the Turks.[116] Their retreat frustrated this plan.

THE DIET OF AUGSBURG

It seems that the prince did not participate at all in the negotiations for the league of the Evangelicals in 1529 and 1530, or at least we know nothing about it, for as his May opinion shows, he certainly did not lack interest in this matter, and his reflections became the basis for the so-called Schwabach Paper and the Saxon instruction for the Diet of Schwabach.[117] He is only referred to as present in person at the meeting of the Protestants in Smalcald from November 28 to December 3, 1529. He again had the opportunity for greater prominence at the Diet of Augsburg.[118] <75> We could even regret that he participated in person, since that means that the excellent resource we have in his 1529 letters disappears! The religious questions were certainly at the forefront of his interest; since we have already referred to what was done with them at the diet and John Frederick's part in that, little remains to be said.

We could certainly expect that the electoral prince would be busily active against the election of Ferdinand, in keeping with his opinion of 1529. What he had feared in that opinion now took place in fact: the emperor made use of the diet to win over the Catholic electors for the election.[119] When we now find no trace of any counteraction from John Frederick, that can be because of the fragmentary nature of our source material, or the prince may have been quickly convinced of the hopelessness of such an attempt. Moreover, it is not to be overlooked that only two electors were personally present, among whom there was from the start no hope of success, the electors of Mainz and

---

Neuenahr (Cornelius 10:155).

115 Beier was to accompany him as councilor, Schurf as physician, according to an August 19, 1529, letter from Rörer to Roth (Buchwald, *Zur Wittenberger Stadt- und Universitätsgeschichte*, 63).

116 Spalatin ap. Menck, 2:1117; Struve 3:165; Ranke 3:142; in Reg. O. No. 24, fol. 83 the relevant passage is crossed out.

117 PC 1:414f. note; J. J. Müller, 285f.

118 Among the documents that were taken to Augsburg, we also find his advice concerning the Turks (Förstemann, *U.*, 1:135).

119 Cf. Winckelmann, 13f.

Brandenburg. In addition, the chief discussions about the election took place after John Frederick's departure from the diet. The idea at that time of excluding Saxony would certainly have provoked the electoral prince's great indignation, for we can make the observation that during the diet, he gave strict attention that the ceremonial rights of the house of Saxony not be infringed. This had especially to be safeguarded at the entrance of the emperor: at the head of the Saxon train, the prince himself led the way, and when at the opening of the diet, the emperor went from the church to the city hall, the electoral princes of Saxony and Brandenburg went ahead of him.[120]

After his return from the diet, John Frederick devoted himself to the problems produced by the proceedings at the diet. Since the emperor began to mobilize, they had to be ready for the worst. The electoral prince also began to be occupied with plans for mobilizing and recruiting. Hans von Dolzig forwarded an opinion on this to him from Augsburg,[121] and John <76> Frederick replied that if necessary, they must certainly do what they can justify before God and conscience.[122] A year before this, he would have written: "before God and His Imperial Majesty." Since then, however, he had become convinced that opposition to the emperor could not be avoided and could even be legally defended.[123] As a result, negotiations for the league naturally claimed new interest. First, however, John Frederick faced a new problem. On December 21, his father was invited by the emperor to talks about important imperial concerns at Cologne, and on the twenty-ninth, he received a summons from the elector of Mainz to the same place for the election of the Roman king. It was to be foreseen that on the twenty-first, only this point would be discussed; since the elector was completely clear that if he were personally present for the election of Ferdinand, nothing more could be changed, he decided to make use of the many violations against the legal provisions that also crept in to protest against the election and declare it invalid.[124] It was natural to entrust this problem to the electoral prince, who had already been occupied for a long time with just this point.

---

120 May 11 letter from John Frederick to Dolzig (CR 2:48f.). J. J. Müller, 562; Schirrmacher, 75; Ranke 3:168.

121 From October 1 (Reg. H., 46, No. 4, fol. 112–22, 123–38).

122 On October 14 (Förstemann, *U.*, 2:735f.).

123 Winckelmann, 36.

124 On the matter of the election, cf. Noack, *Die Exception Sachsens von der Wahl Ferdinands I.* (program, Krefeld, 1886), and Winckelmann, 19f., 58f. Both are in need of much correcting and supplementing. I made use of the December 4 instruction for John Frederick (Loc. 10671 "Concerning the Election of King Ferdinand," 1531), the detailed Saxon report on the election (Loc. 10671 "Schreiben und Bedenken"), and the letters from John Frederick to John (Loc. 10671).

JOHN FREDERICK PROTESTS IN COLOGNE AGAINST THE ELECTION OF FERDINAND

He set out on December 4 accompanied by Hans von Minkwitz, Hans von Dolzig, Taubenheim, Groß, and Spalatin; they stopped in Spangenberg on December 11/12 with the Count of Hesse. John Frederick had Minkwitz report to him in detail about the election, and Philip expressed his joy that there was still a devout elector in the empire.[125] The electoral prince arrived in Cologne on December 19, and on the twentieth, he had an audience <77> with the emperor in the presence of King Ferdinand, the Cardinal of Lüttich, Count Palatine Friedrich, the Margrave of Arschot, Mr. von Praet, and the imperial secretary Alexander Schweiß. Hans von Minkwitz spoke for Saxony and explained that the elector who had received the invitation on November 28 could not come because of the distance, his age, and his infirmity, and so he and John Frederick were to represent him. In Saxony, they had feared that the emperor would not be satisfied with this excuse, but after a brief consultation, Charles had Count Palatine Friedrich tell the Saxon delegates that he would accept them for negotiations with the elector. These negotiations began on December 24, and the speculation that they would deal only with the question of the election was soon shown to be correct. The emperor had it explained to the assembled electors that because of his other lands, he could not always be in the empire, but that during his absence in the present dangerous times, "much offense" could happen, and for that reason, he asked them to elect his brother Ferdinand as Roman king. To a request the electors made to the emperor on December 26 that he would remain in the empire,[126] he repeated his wish that his brother would be elected, and now the Catholic electors joined the discussions about the election. When they now as a formality asked the emperor for a free election (in reality, they had long since all been gained for Ferdinand), they reached the limit to which the Saxon ambassadors could go in keeping with their instructions. Saxony took its stand on the strictly legal viewpoint that the emperor was not to set an election day. John Frederick and Minkwitz only had the authority to participate in discussions about other imperial business, insofar as they could be attended to by the elector without the remaining

125 Instructions for the negotiations with Philip (Loc. 10671 "Concerning the Election of King Ferdinand"); a report of one of the councilors on the negotiations (Loc. 10671 "Concerning the Election of King Ferdinand"; Winckelmann, 50).

126 Between the twenty-fourth and the twenty-sixth, John Frederick could have separately negotiated with the electors. In his instructions, he had been directed to conduct such negotiations with the Palatinate and Trier, but there is nothing about this in the Saxon report on the election.

estates, but not in discussions about the election. Naturally, they could not be dissuaded from this by anything the emperor said. The emperor's conclusive permission <78> for a free election made it possible for the Saxon representatives to participate in the discussions, since they were no longer negotiating with the emperor about the election. These discussions began on the twenty-eighth, and here Electoral Saxony naturally brought up the reflections against undertaking the election of a king that had partially been developed in 1529 by John Frederick. These noted that the election of the Roman king was not mentioned in the Golden Bull; it is questionable whether this really belongs to the rights of the electors; the offense of the emperor's capitulation in the election, in which he bound himself to remain in the empire; the danger that some time the emperor and the king could at the same time claim the support of the empire for different purposes; the difficulty that they must serve two lords; and the dangerous consequences this could have for every illegal activity in these already agitated times.

Naturally, these ideas had no effect; rather, the remaining electors decided to take the necessary steps to begin discussing the election on the next day. On this day, the second part of the instructions to the Saxon ambassadors came into force. Saxony could only accomplish something with its opposition to the election if it did not participate at all in it and then declared it to be invalid. This was made easier by what their adversaries did. They did not at all need to insist on their contention that the Golden Bull does not speak about the election of a Roman king during the lifetime of the emperor, since Charles IV had himself repudiated that. By summoning Saxony, the elector of Mainz had violated the formalities, since the prescribed period of three months was not allowed. In addition, there was the arbitrary change of the place of the election. Saxony therefore declared the summons to be void; it was the same as if the elector had not been invited at all, and therefore the electors have to refrain from the election. If they nevertheless carry on the election, Saxony will protest against it and declare it to be invalid.

This was the content of the Electoral Saxon protest that John Frederick and Minkwitz submitted to the elector of Mainz on December 29, which they wanted read to the assembly if the other electors had not refused permission for this in spite of <79> their request repeated three times. They had to be satisfied with a solemn, verbal protest. The electors certainly did not let this prevent them from carrying out the election, but the actions of Electoral Saxony were the reason this was delayed until January 5, 1531.[127] Naturally, however, all the

127 The "exemption" had already taken place on the twenty-seventh, so that cannot have delayed the election. The delegates from Nuremberg took the view that it was the fault of the Saxon protest.

counter-protests, declarations, and alliances of the electors that could have been discussed in the meantime[128] could not do away with Saxony's legally justified protest, and the electoral prince saw to it that this was known in the widest possible circles. On the thirtieth, he sent a copy to Count Wilhelm von Nassau and asked him to share it with Count Wilhelm von Neuenahr, Philip of Solms, and others, for they wanted many people to know about this.[129] John Frederick seems also to have shared the official document with the Nuremberg delegates Tetzel and Koler in Cologne. They sent "the writing" home and confidently expected that it would be forwarded from there to others.[130] In general, Saxony had now by its actions obtained a firm legal basis from which it could in the future with good conscience refuse to recognize Ferdinand as king and be the focus of opposition to him.

If we cast a glance at the personal attitude of John Frederick in Cologne, he did not have all that much opportunity to come into prominence, since Hans von Minkwitz was the spokesman in the name of Electoral Saxony. This was certainly based on ceremonial usages; there can be no doubt about the electoral prince's complete agreement with the standard politics of Saxony. This is shown by his letters from this time. It is clear from these letters that he was not for a moment in doubt that Ferdinand would be elected and that he was also completely clear about the reasons for this; to him, the empire <80> seemed to have been "miserably sold," and the efforts for a free election were only "putting on a mask."[131] Actually, compared to the dissimulation of the electors, the attitude of Saxony that was not completely influenced by selfish motives made a pleasant impression; it also obviously took some courage to oppose the emperor in such a direct way. I have not been able to establish whether the rumor that right after his departure from Cologne, the electoral prince was waylaid is based on truth or not.[132]

John Frederick and Minkwitz departed from Cologne already on December 29, leaving behind a written apology for the emperor.[133] They went to Hambach to the electoral prince's parents-in-law. From there, he still sought to have influence on the further developments of the election. He forbade Marshal

---

128 Noack, 12; there could also have been discussions about the capitulation from the election.

129 Loc. 10671 "Concerning the Election of King Ferdinand," 1531.

130 January 3, 1531, letter from Tetzel and Koler to John Frederick (Loc. 10671 "Concerning the Election of King Ferdinand," original).

131 (*"ein nassen machen."*—Tr.) December 28 letter to John (Loc. 10671 "Concerning the Election of King Ferdinand," 1531, handwritten; Official Document No. 22; see p. 137 <136>).

132 Loesche, *Analecta*, 197, No. 302. The electoral prince mentions nothing of the kind in his letters.

133 The French version is in Lanz, *Korresp.*, 1:414f.; the German version is in the Saxon report on the election.

Georg Wolf von Pappenheim to serve the king,[134] but he scarcely achieved great results with that. Nikolaus Meier kept him up-to-date on the coronation proceedings at Aachen.[135]

FEDERATION PROCEEDINGS

However, his chief problem in Hambach was to get his father-in-law to take a definite stand in the conflict now expected at any time; he could not get him to do more than make the weak statement that if the elector were unfairly burdened, he would speak with his estates and do the right thing.[136] Even in the matter of the election, John Frederick could not obtain any kind of a binding statement from the prince of Jülich-Cleves.[137] From Hambach, John Frederick then returned home through Hesse; he arrived home in time to attend the Diet of Zwickau. The chief <81> interest now, however, was claimed by the conclusion of the Protestant league. When he had journeyed to Cologne, John Frederick had delivered to the count a summons to a meeting of the Evangelicals in Smalcald; this had then taken place during the negotiations at Cologne, and from Cologne, the electoral prince had followed the deliberations with interest. Because of the rumors about a council and certain threatening statements from Ferdinand, a "constitution for defense" now seemed urgently necessary to him.[138] He recommended that if they could not now reach that goal, they set a new date before the Saxon diet and conclude things there, for they "dare not rest now."[139] Because of the ambassadors of the cities, it was not possible to fulfill this wish.[140] But the Protestant estates did meet anew in Smalcald in February 1531, and on the twenty-seventh, the Smalcald League was concluded. John Frederick also subscribed this, although nothing is known about his participation in these final negotiations.

In order to arrange and organize the league further, numerous meetings of the league were soon necessary, and John Frederick repeatedly acted as representative for his father at these; however, he was so strictly bound to the instructions given him that we cannot with full certainty conclude anything

---

134 January 6, 1531, letter to John (Loc. 10671 "Schreiben und Bedenken").

135 January 13 letter from Meier to John Frederick (Loc. 10672, "Writings between Saxony, Bavaria, etc.").

136 Below 1:201f.

137 April 29, 1531, letter from John at Torgau to Wildenfels (Loc. 10672 "Writings . . . ," original).

138 December 28 letter to John (Loc. 10671 "Concerning the Election of King Ferdinand"; Official Document No. 22; see p. 137 <136>).

139 December 28 and 29 letters to John (Loc. 10671, "Schreiben und Bedenken").

140 January 1 letter from John to John Frederick (Loc. 10671 "Concerning the Election of King Ferdinand," 1531).

from his actions about his views. This applies, for example, to the question already treated in the previous chapter about accepting the Swiss into the league. At the Diet of Smalcald, which took place in April 1531, the elector gave his son a special warning only to engage in mobilization and recruiting troops if all the members of the league agreed, so that they would not under the appearance of defense be led by the count into a revolt.[141] From this, it can perhaps be concluded that at the Saxon court, the prince was always regarded as the advocate of the war party. <82> In fact, during his stay in Hambach in January, he had already made arrangements with cavalrymen; he left 410 florins there so that Gangolf von Heilingen, who had been sent to Jülich on April 3 about the election, could easily make further arrangements.[142] Many other things also indicate that the prince regarded especially the military side of the league as his profession. We have some "Reflections" from him dated November 11 and 13, 1531, in which he is occupied almost exclusively with military arrangements, which the constitution of the league made necessary in the Saxon regions.[143] At that time, they were afraid of war, as it appears from some letters of the count; on November 14, commands were issued to the captains and officials to hold themselves in readiness.[144] Also with reference to the constitution of the league, it was the military and financial questions that most interested John Frederick; at least, he was only occupied with them in some articles that the prince drew up toward the end of 1531 on the "arrangement for defense." The goal of the somewhat obscure document was greater promptness in raising and increasing the monthly subscriptions of the members of the league in time of war.[145] From all of this, however, we can no longer conclude that these aspects of the proceedings especially enticed the electoral prince to express his own opinions. We do not know how he collaborated in organizing the league through participation in the meetings of the league, at the meetings of the Saxon councilors, and through other verbal discussions. He did at least once express himself in writing about the value of the constitution of the Smalcald League and stated that "a better constitution" could not be devised. Therefore, it was his opinion that they should make it the basis for establishing a league opposed to the election of Ferdinand.[146]

---

141 March 25 letter from John at Torgau to John Frederick (Reg. H., 46, No. 4, fol. 38/39).

142 Loc. 10672 "Writings, etc." 1531; April 5, 1531, letter from John Frederick at Georgenthal to John (Reg. H., 59, No. 13, fol. 25f.); John's answer on the eighth (Reg. H., 46, No. 4, fol. 107f.).

143 Reg. H., 54, No. 9.

144 Loc. 10671 "Concerning the Election of King Ferdinand," 1531.

145 Reg. H., 61, No. 14, fol. 39–41.

146 According to the October 18, 1531, instructions for Minkwitz and Dolzig to be mentioned later (Loc.

THE FEDERATION OF THOSE AGAINST THE ELECTION

<83> The leaders of Saxon politics would have liked it best if all the members of the Smalcald League had together declared their opposition to the recognition of Ferdinand. Since the cities did not favor this opposition, but the election was strongly contested by the Catholic princes of Bavaria, there was need to form, in addition to the Smalcald League, a separate league of those opposed to the election. The negotiations about this proceeded so well by the fall of 1531 that they expected to conclude the league in October at a meeting of ambassadors called for Saalfeld.[147] When Saxony was taking the necessary steps to prepare for the Diet of Saalfeld, the only Saxon councilors in on this—Minkwitz, Brück, and Dolzig—proposed to the elector that he induce his son to give his opinion.[148] Because of this, we have John Frederick's handwritten draft of instructions for the councilors Minkwitz and Dolzig, who were to be sent to Saalfeld.[149] We learn from this that the electoral prince regarded the election league to be nothing but an extension of the Smalcald League; he even recommended that the Smalcald constitution serve as the basis for the election constitution. With reference to the question of the election, he persisted in his strictly legal view and rejected any election of an opposition king. Since the election of a Roman king did not conform to the Golden Bull, he was inclined to enter into far-reaching international relations, above all with England, France, and Denmark for support against the election.

With unessential changes, John Frederick's draft was the basis for the instruction the two ambassadors actually then received, and we again often find John Frederick's proposals in the October 24 settlement of the Saalfeld League.[150] So it was in part <84> his own special task at which he had the opportunity to work further in the spring of 1532. Not just after the death of his father but already since March 1532, the threads of all Saxon politics ran through his hands. The negotiations with the emperor for peace that were already taking place in the spring of 1531 were what provided him with this prominent role on the political stage.

10671 "Concerning the Election of King Ferdinand," 1531).

147 The details are in Winckelmann.

148 October 2 memorial of these three (Loc. 10671?).

149 Loc. 10671 "Concerning the Election of King Ferdinand," 1531, handwritten draft; Loc. 10672 "Schriften," has the dispatch used by Winckelmann.

150 Stumpf, *Politische Geschichte Bayerns*, I, Appendix, No. IV, 16; Neudecker, *Merkwürdige Aktenstücke*, 68f.

THE NEGOTIATIONS FOR PEACE

After Charles V had fallen into severe opposition to Electoral Saxony during the proceedings at Cologne, he had to be convinced that the general political situation made vigorous action against the Protestants for the time being impossible for him, and that even coming to terms with them was desirable. Therefore, he was not reluctant to agree to the proposal of the electors of Mainz and the Palatinate to take up the negotiations.[151] Their undertaking was parallel to a second of Counts Wilhelm von Nassau and Wilhelm von Neuenahr, who seemed especially suitable for the restoration of peace because of their close connections to both sides. Even if similar attempts that they had already made in 1530 had been frustrated by imperial politics, they were still ready in the summer of 1531 to repeat their efforts by all means on the basis of precise instructions.[152] They, as well as the two electors, were commanded to bring about a settlement in the religious question and in the business of the election. This depended above all on gaining Saxony and Hesse, and so the mediators were directed to negotiate with the electoral prince as well as with the elector, proof of the influence ascribed to him already then. Right at the beginning, the negotiations were partially carried out by him. At the beginning of June, he met with the two electors or their ambassadors,[153] and he was present in August when the two counts delivered the emperor's propositions to the elector in Weimar. John even in part left the negotiations to him, <85> and we can assume that the answer given to the counts corresponded throughout with his views. It was just as little in his character as in that of his father to be won over through personal compromises, and the emperor's efforts in this regard could have as little results as in the question of the confirmation of the marriage, on which John Frederick was most dependent; his goodwill had to be won through lasting good conduct toward Electoral Saxony. It was certainly because of John Frederick that the elector most decisively rejected every connection with the Anabaptists. The demand for the freedom to preach and to eat meat on fast days as a condition for attending the imperial diet corresponded completely with the demands John Frederick had approved of already in his letters of 1529. The declaration that granting aid against the Turks can only be thought of after the previous guarantee of inner peace calls directly to mind

151 Lanz, *Korresp.*, 1:429f., 444, 447.

152 Lanz, *Korresp.*, 1:510–16.

153 I take this from Burkhardt, *Landtagsakten*, 1:247, No. 450, but I can say nothing more specific about it.

the statements of the electoral prince at that time; it is obvious that he did not think of any flexibility in the question of the election.[154]

Thus it was certainly thanks to the young prince when both counts had to depart with their mission completely unaccomplished. In spite of that, the negotiations were not abandoned. The electors of Mainz and the Palatinate continued it, but now they met with very little cooperation from the Protestants. When a delegate conference took place in Smalcald on September 1, the Protestant representatives only had the authority to listen and report back.[155] In Saxony, they seem to have thought it possible that the emperor would approve the Saxon conditions for attending the diet, for in a September 29 letter that John Frederick directed to the count of Neuenahr and in which he inquired about the status of the negotiations with the emperor, he referred to certain warnings about the threat of danger at the diet and asked the count to investigate this.[156] <86> He answered on October 15 that he and the count of Nassau knew nothing about these supposed dangers, but that he would be on the alert. In the business with the emperor, again nothing had happened, since the emperor had his hopes on the diet and on the activity of the two electors.[157] In fact, they continued their efforts through the whole winter, but we do not need to enter into any further details here, since John Frederick did not in any way stand out in this.[158] The final result was that a meeting of the Evangelicals with the two electors was arranged for March 30 in Schweinfurt. An attempt would be made there to achieve peace. Now, since they would also use this opportunity to put the finishing touches on the constitution of the Smalcald League, and since from Schweinfurt the negotiations with the Bavarian princes on the election league and its expansion would eagerly be continued, we find John Frederick connected to the three great political actions in which Electoral Saxony was involved. He represented his father at all these negotiations and was becoming a very important person.

SCHWEINFURT

Of course, his role was carefully prescribed for him by detailed instructions; we do not know if he had any part in preparing those instructions. Should the

154 Sleidan, fol. 125/26; Neudecker, *Merkwürdige Aktenstücke*, 1:58–66; Lanz, *Korresp.*, 1:512–16, 523–28; Winckelmann, 138f. A Saxon record of the negotiations is in Reg. H, 50, No. 5, fol. 60–65.

155 Lanz, *Korresp.*, 1:530–33.

156 Draft in his own hand (Reg. H. 50, No. 5, fol. 89/90; Official Document No. 23; see p. 138 <137>).

157 Handwritten (Reg. H. 50, No. 5, fol. 91–93, 95).

158 Cf. Winckelmann, 175f.

case arise, he had the authority to agree or to refuse together with the other allies, insofar as that could happen without burdening their consciences. He needed to report first to the elector only if he had to decide whether to go to the diet, which the emperor had in the meantime summoned to Regensburg.[159] There, Saxony was represented at first only by ambassadors; at the request of John Frederick, they were instructed to receive their orders from him.[160] This would guarantee the consistency of Saxon politics. The instructions John Frederick gave reveal the principles that controlled Saxon politics and at the same time demonstrate <87> that the fears harbored especially by Count Philip that Saxony would be too flexible were unfounded. The idea, of course, suggested itself of meeting the emperor halfway on the election question in order to obtain concessions in the area of religion; this idea was completely absent from the perhaps too correct and conscientious Saxon politicians. John Frederick was instructed always to keep the two negotiations separate because Bavaria shared in the opposition to the election; he strictly enforced this and finally compelled the mediators to comply with his wishes.

Since we have already treated the main point about the settlement of the religious controversy elsewhere, here we will go into the matter of the election in somewhat more detail. The electoral prince had received very detailed instructions on this point. According to those instructions, he was first to call for the king to divest himself of the title he had acquired through the illegal election. If the emperor then desired an election, he should first fill the gap contained in the Golden Bull in this regard, since he with the imperial estates made additions to it. Saxony would gladly cooperate with this; indeed, a draft for this manifesto[161] was inserted into the instructions of the prince. If the emperor would not agree to annul the election, then an impartial verdict should settle the controversy. If that could not be achieved, then the two electors could get permission for the elector of Saxony to present in open audience before the assembled estates the reasons why the election could not be certified. Nevertheless, they were also finally ready to yield to a request of the emperor because of his honor and for the sake of peace that the election should be certified, if the other participants agreed and if that manifesto was added to the Golden Bull. This approval, however, would not really be recognition of the

---

159 Dated March 20 (Loc. 10672 "What was done at Schweinfurt," fol. 1–30, original).

160 April 1 letter from John Frederick to John (Reg. H., 63, No. 16, vol. 1, fol. 105f.); John's April 7 answer (Reg. H., 63, No. 16, vol. 2, fol. 29–31).

161 To be found in Goldast, *Politische Reichshändel*, 144/145; this was not used in any way.

election of Ferdinand, but they would obey him as an assistant to the emperor and would be obliged to him after the death of the emperor.

<88> John Frederick did not have much opportunity to make use of these instructions, since Bavaria could not be persuaded to participate in the Diet of Schweinfurt, and therefore, he could only conduct informal negotiations with the electors on the election question. The attempt of the two electors to win over Saxony by fulfilling its specific desires with reference to granting a fief and establishing an annual fair in Gotha also did not meet with success. John Frederick did not at all intend to separate from his allies. However, it was doubtless his opinion that a compromise on the election question could not be prevented by the opposition of a single member of the league. He got into a heated correspondence on this with Count Philip who would not yield to a majority decision. On the whole, it was a pointless controversy, since what they assumed did not happen; rather, they resolved to hold a meeting of the opponents of the election in Nuremberg on what was to be done further.

Before we go into these later incidents, we will take a comprehensive glance at John Frederick's activity in Schweinfurt. The first thing we stress is that he zealously took part in the difficult discussions; he also assisted on the committees that were chosen for various occasions. His state of mind at the beginning was not very hopeful. "We have little hope that anything fruitful will be done here," he wrote on April 1.[162] Prospects got better by the middle of the month,[163] but on the twenty-fourth, he again used almost the same words.[164] He was not dissatisfied with the final outcome of the discussions.[165] When they did not reach a conclusion, there was still hope that at the new diet, which was to take place in Nuremberg, the electors would be provided with instructions from Charles to continue.

Only a little can be said about the participation of John Frederick in the discussions that were held at Schweinfurt on the organization of the Smalcald League. Surely he was delighted that the "arrangement <89> for defense" was finally concluded here, and his choice as leader along with Philip of Hesse was certainly to his liking, given his military inclinations.[166]

The electoral prince made use of the interval before the resumption of the peace discussions for a journey to Torgau and Wittenberg and for the

---

162 Letter to John (Reg. H., 63, No. 16, vol. 1, fol. 105f.).

163 April 19 instructions for Minkwitz (Reg. A. No. 247).

164 Letter to John (Reg. H. 63, No. 16, vol. 3, fol. 31–36).

165 May 4 letter to Neuenahr (Cornelius 10:137f.); May 7 letter to John (Reg. H. 63, No. 16, fol. 109; Official Document No. 24; see p. 139 <139>).

166 Cf. PC 2:134, 136f.; Winckelmann, 210f.; Reg. H. No. 16, vol. 3, fol. 104–8.

consultation with the theologians mentioned before. In addition, at this time, he was busy attending to conferences with the members of the election league. Nothing came of the meeting planned between John Frederick, Count Philip, and the princes of Bavaria or their ambassadors in Nuremberg; on the contrary, the representatives of the three princes met on May 8 at Königsberg in Franconia. Saxony was represented by Brück and Minkwitz. The discussions had important results for the organization of the league; they spoke about relations with John Zápolya and with France, drew up an "arrangement for defense," but did not at all speak about the peace negotiations.[167] Most important of all these concerns was the negotiation with France. However, Minkwitz and Brück did not have full authority for that, and so the conclusion of the negotiations had to be postponed to a new meeting in Munich. Hans von Minkwitz journeyed there, while Brück set out for Torgau. From there, instructions on which John Frederick collaborated, according to Brück's testimony, were forwarded to Minkwitz.[168] It is interesting that they thought they had to take precautions not to get entangled through the league in France's selfish endeavors or forced into a war of aggression. Furthermore, the Saxon desire to continue the peace <90> negotiations in the matter of the election again became very prominent. The ambassador was to work at getting them to make a definite decision "on which they finally intend safely to persevere in the matter of the election of the king or what compromises they can tolerate in it."

We do not know how far Minkwitz fulfilled these directions, since no details are known about the negotiations carried out from May 26 on at Scheyern Abbey in Munich. There were very heated debates especially on the twenty-eighth and twenty-ninth, both among the German representatives and between them and the French ambassador du Bellay.[169] Finally on May 31,[170] the princes of the election league agreed with France on a league for "the defense and maintenance of German freedom." Since the matter of the election was not even mentioned there, we can scarcely imagine that Saxony consented to this agreement that could lead to dangerous consequences.

---

167 Instruction for Minkwitz and Brück (Loc. 10672 "Handlung und Abschied zu Königsberg"); a transcript of the discussions is in Stumpf, *Urkundenb.* No. 5:20–28; May 11 report of Minkwitz and Brück to John Frederick (Loc. 10672, op. cit.).

168 May 18 letter from Brück to Minkwitz (Reg. H. 65, No. 17, vol. 1, fol. 5); the instructions (Loc. 10672 "Handlung und Abschied," original); I have not been able to locate the copy in John Frederick's hand that Winckelmann (note 433) mentions.

169 According to Minkwitz's May 30 report (Loc. 10672 "Handlung und Abschied").

170 The Friday after Corpus Christi, according to a copy of the agreement (Loc. 10672 "Handlung und Abschied").

NURREMBERG

John Frederick received Minkwitz's report in Nuremberg, where he had arrived on June 3 for the resumption of the peace negotiations. We have already dealt with the more important side of these negotiations, namely, the religious side. The election business was only continued with difficulty, since Bavaria again was not represented; nevertheless, it had a decisive effect on Saxon politics that the emperor now decided to agree to the complete separation of this question from the negotiations about religious peace. They were still working at expanding the election league, but the Saxons found no sympathy in the princes of Bavaria in support of the request of Prince Albrecht of Prussia for reception into the league.[171] The count of Hesse's and their efforts to reach a settlement with John Zápolya[172] were strangely in opposition to John Frederick's inclination to participate in the war on the Turks. He thought that when the Protestants made peace <91> with the emperor, they could no longer justly refuse to furnish help against the Turks. He recommended that they make the preparations necessary for this before peace was established, sent to the elector detailed opinions about the measures they should take, sent Albrecht of Belzig into the Danube region to investigate the situation there, and kept busy himself with recruiting.[173] His enthusiasm was certainly not very political, since their opponents very much depended on the support of the Protestants in the war on the Turks,[174] and therefore they could still obtain many concessions from them by greater restraint in this area.

John Frederick's behavior was certainly influenced by the hope he had in mind that he himself could play a role in the war on the Turks; he was counting on a command position and was somewhat hurt when those on the emperor's side did not offer this to him.[175] Perhaps these were the "other matters" that caused the Hessian chancellor Feige to question the altruism of Saxon politics.[176] There could be more justice in the reproach Philip of Hesse made that he was influenced by questions that had only an indirect connection with

---

171 June 17 letter from John Frederick to the princes of Bavaria (Reg. H., 65, No. 17, vol. 1, fol. 113f.); June 14 copy to John (ibid., fol. 90–94, original); June 21 letter from the princes of Bavaria to John Frederick (ibid., vol. 2, fol. 407, copy); and often.

172 That is, the king of Hungary (1526–40).—Tr.

173 Nearly every letter from John Frederick to John in June and July speaks about the Turks; cf. in addition the June 19 instruction for Belzig (Reg. H., 65, No. 17, vol. 2, fol. 29–31); June 26 instruction for Minkwitz to John (Reg. H., 65, No. 17, vol. 2, fol. 57–66).

174 Cf. Ficker, 604f. 618; Lanz, *Korresp.* 1:679–81.

175 July 28 letter from John Frederick to Neuenahr (Cornelius 10:151; cf. also Rommel 1:313).

176 Wille, 81f. The efforts of the cardinal of Trent to win over John Frederick naturally came too late (Förstemann, *U.*, 2:125f.).

the present negotiations. John Frederick and Brück were not for a moment in doubt that much of Hesse's opposition to the peace would be removed if the Württemberg and Nassau affairs were settled.[177] <92> Just this view of Hessian politics shows why they were so incensed at the Hessian doubt of their loyalty to the league, the reproaches in Philip's letters, and the difficulties their councilors made at the negotiations. It was not completely without justice that they regarded the count as the opponent of peace, and as a result, the detailed suspicions he raised lost some of their effect.

It is well-known that this opposition in the summer of 1532 furnished the occasion for a very sharp correspondence between Philip and John.[178] There was also correspondence between the landgrave and John Frederick. It began in March with the efforts of Philip to prevent the prince from attending the Diet of Schweinfurt; on March 25, his chancellor Feige received very odd instructions that, among other things, he should hold out to John Frederick the prospect of the Roman kingship.[179] This attempt, however, seems to have been rather ineffective on the electoral prince.[180] Then in Schweinfurt, it was especially the Hessian councilors who raised objections to Saxon politics; there was also a correspondence between Philip and John Frederick on the legality of majority decisions in the election affair. Nothing good for the interest of unity came from a meeting of both princes proposed in May; in the summer, John Frederick was also dragged into the correspondence of his father with the landgrave. We find that John had his son and the councilors in Nuremberg draw up an answer to something the landgrave had written, which, according to John Frederick's phrase, contained "some very troublesome words."[181] From the end of July on, the correspondence was then taken over by John Frederick. On July 29, he sought to justify in detail Saxony's viewpoint. The answer was a very characteristic but also very blunt writing from the landgrave.[182] John Frederick thought that the <93> insults contained in it should not be left unanswered,

---

177 Cf. besides Wille, 71f., the April 9 letter from Brück in Schweinfurt to John: "I think that if the Nassau and Württemberg matters had taken a different form, then no one would have been more charitable on the other matters than my lord the count" (Reg. H., 63, No. 16, vol. 2, fol. 54, handwritten); July 9 letter from John Frederick in Nuremberg to John: "But I think that if the Nassau affair could be resolved peaceably, there would be no trouble in dealing with the count" (Reg. H., 65, No. 17, vol. 3, fol. 58–60, original); Official Document No. 27; see p. 142 <141>.

178 Seckendorf 3:22f.

179 March 25 instruction for Feige (Reg. H., 63, No. 16, vol. 1).

180 April 5 instruction from John Frederick for Anark von Wildenfels (Reg. H., 63, No. 16, vol. 2, fol. 11–18, draft in Brück's handwriting).

181 June 14 letter to John (Reg. H., 65, No. 17, vol. 1, fol. 90, 94, original).

182 Copies of both letters (Reg. H., 70, No. 19; cf. Seckendorf, op. cit.); John Frederick called Philip's letter "awkward, unkind, angry, and harsh" in an August 5 letter to John.

but it was also clear to him that any continuation of the correspondence could only lead to unpleasant complications; therefore, he proposed to his father already on August 5 that the controversy should be settled by the councilors on each side.[183] Carrying out this idea was one of the first actions of John Frederick after his accession, and we will have to return to it later.

183 Reg. H., 63, No. 16, vol. 4, fol. 125–26.

Conclusion

Our presentation has scarcely given us a complete picture of the activity of John Frederick before his accession, since the material available does not give us information on all the questions that could be raised. It has, however, shown us one thing, namely, that on August 16, 1532, the prince was well prepared in every respect to ascend the Saxon electoral throne. He possessed understanding and interest in the intellectual aspirations of his time; he had acquired a definite viewpoint and position on the chief question that stirred hearts, the religious question, even though he did not completely renounce his independence toward the opinions of the theologians. In the area of politics, he had obtained experience on many sides, a penetrating knowledge of all the chief questions, and an extensive knowledge of the people involved.

Immediately after the death of John the Steadfast, Luther is said to have pronounced a remarkable verdict on the new elector: "Wisdom died with Prince Frederick and piety with Prince John; from now on, the nobility that ignores wisdom and piety will rule." The young lord would have his own mind and would not pay much attention to the pen. He is certainly clever enough, but his own willfulness and the influence of the nobility will form a dangerous counterweight to it.[1] If we ask how far our investigations so far confirm this verdict of the certainly well-informed Luther, then it is certainly undeniable that John Frederick did not possess the wise prudence that was characteristic of his uncle; but we are more surprised that Luther deprives him of piety. We <94> can perhaps suspect that this verdict is expressing Luther's feeling based on past experiences that the influence of the theologians will be less under the new elector than in the past. Luther's idea that the nobility would have too great an influence on John Frederick seems to have been shared by John the Steadfast when in his August 25, 1529, testament, he warned his son not to be misled by "devilish councilors."[2] If we ask whether this verdict was justified, it

1 Alt. 5:1030.
2 Reg. D. 141.

is immediately notable that John Frederick occasionally expressed very similar ideas with reference to his father.[3] Just as he generally was not satisfied with the "old government," since for him everything went too slow, this prudence stirred up his nature, which was not yet completely sluggish but still somewhat impetuous and impatient. He did have an especially friendly relationship with some of his father's noble councilors, such as Hans von Minkwitz, Hans von Dolzig, and perhaps even Anark von Wildenfels. This gives us the opportunity to observe that this is not evidence that he was dangerously dependent on them. The record of his own governance as elector can clarify for us how far Luther's verdict was correct. But in order not to leave this with such a gloomy outlook, we can contrast Luther's verdict with that of someone who knew the young prince well, Count Wilhelm von Neuenahr, who wrote to the prince on June 6, 1532, to remain in his Christian, honorable, German ways. "For we unfortunately have no one we can regard as a father of the German Fatherland in divine and human affairs except for Your Princely Grace's father and Your Princely Grace."[4] <95>

---

3 March 20, 1529, letter from John Frederick to Brück (Loc. 10671 "Schreiben und Bedenken," fol. 28, rough draft in his own hand).

4 Cornelius 10:141.

OFFICIAL DOCUMENTS[1]

1. A list of the treasures, clothes, and other things of my gracious young lord Prince Hans Frederick, which were present at the departure of Teacher Alexius Colditz [Michaelmas 1519].[2]

First, all kinds of treasures are listed, among which are a silver picture of Mary hanging from an Our Father, a small Our Father on which there are five gilded standards and five flaps with a red phylactery, on which there is the angelic greeting, . . . a gilded statue of St. Anne. *Of the other property, these are perhaps worthy of note*: a small, gilded, covered cup with an acorn on the lid from which my gracious young lord would drink each day; two swords; three battle swords; ten knives short and long, six with silver handles; a hunting dagger with a twist.

We finish with my gracious young lord's books in Latin and German.

Latin Books

Bibles, a large Terence, a small Terence,[3] the *Education of Christian Princes* by Erasmus of Rotterdam,[4] the letters of Chrysostom to his teacher Libanius,[5] sermons on the Gospels,[6] Aldus's *Instruction*,[7] Brassicanus's *Grammar*,[8] the apprenticeship of the best prince written by my gracious young lord in his own hand, and the beginnings of Greek compounds[9] also written by my gracious young lord with his own gracious hand. The rules of Latin and Greek grammar written by Teacher Alexius Crosner Colditz, the principles

1 The Official Documents were printed with their original German spelling, which varied considerably from what is common now. These documents are translated with many a guess from the context. The italicized words are Mentz's summary of portions of the documents he omitted.—Tr.

2 Reg. D. No. 148, used on pp. 23f. <9>, 42 <30>.

3 The editions can scarcely be determined.

4 Erasmus, *Institutio boni principiis* (Basel, 1518).

5 Purchased on Michaelmas 1518 (Reg. Bb. 4252; Hain, *Rep.* No. 10069).

6 Perhaps Hain, No. 13305 (Paris, 1500).

7 That is, *Institutionum grammaticarum libri quatuor* (published in 1516 by the firm of Aldus Manutius [1449–1515] in Venice); J. Müller, 257.

8 Johannes Brassicanus (1475–1514), *Institutiones grammaticae* (1508 and often); Jöcher 1:1342; J. Müller, 269f.

9 *Rudimenta graecanica et parasintheta* = parasynthesis.—Tr.

of a prince, a vocabulary, the course of the Roman Church,[10] the *Garden of the Soul*,[11] the course of St. Bonaventure,[12] the passion of our Lord Jesus Christ with pictures,[13] and the acts of Dr. Martin Luther at Augsburg.[14]

<96> In all, nineteen Latin books. Among these books, three are still to be bound, which will cost eighteen groschen.

German Books

The rules of the prince, covered with brown velvet and with silver clasps;[15] two German passions with pictures; one German passion with pictures;[16] legends of the saints, both winter and summer parts in two books;[17] a plenarium of the Gospels and of the office of the Holy Mass;[18] the seven penitential psalms of Dr. Martin Luther at Wittenberg;[19] Dr. Martin's exposition of Psalm 110;[20] Dr. Martin's sermon on the meditation on the suffering of Christ divided into fifteen articles;[21] vindication of some articles by Dr. Martin, Augustinian;[22] Dr. Martin's sermon on the Most Holy Sacrament and meditation on the suffering of Christ;[23] the Roman historian Livy;[24] Vegetius on maneuvers;[25] "Parzival"; a collection of medieval heroic poems;[26] Turkish ebronica;[27] a book on fencing;[28] and a large Terence in German.[29]

---

10 Perhaps a liturgical work.

11 *Hortulus animae*, available in so many editions that it is not possible to determine this more exactly.

12 Perhaps *Cursus de passione domini*; cf. Oudin, *Comm. de script. eccl.*, 3:387.

13 *Passio domini nostri Jesu Christi cum figuris*, available in so many editions that it is not possible to determine this more exactly.

14 *Proceedings at Augsburg*, 1518 (LW 31:253–92).

15 I have not been able to identify this.

16 *Passion mit figuren*, available in so many editions that it is not possible to determine this more exactly.

17 *Legenden der lieben hailigen*, available in so many editions that it is not possible to determine this more exactly.

18 Weller, No. 1070, *Das Plenarium oder Evangelibuch* . . . (Basel, 1517).

19 Dommer, Nos. 2, 4, 39; WA 1:154f.

20 Dommer, Nos. 29, 49; WA 1:687f.

21 Dommer, Nos. 62–65; WA 2:131f.; LW 42:3–14.

22 Perhaps Dr. Martin Luther's *Instruction on Some Articles* (WA 2:66f.).

23 Probably Dommer, Nos. 15–17: A good, comforting sermon, etc. (WA 1:325f.).

24 Mainz, 1514.

25 *De re militari*, or in translation *On Knighthood*; Hain, No. 15916.

26 Cf. Goedeke, *Grundriß* I^2, 273f.

27 *Die Turkisch Chronica* (Straßburg, 1516); Weller, No. 991.

28 I cannot identify this book more exactly.

29 Perhaps Hain, No. 15434 of 1499, fol.

2. December 24, 1519, letter from John in Hummelshain to John Frederick. An admonition to go to the Holy Sacrament.[30]

My dear son, we have written that you should go to the Most Holy Sacrament in the morning, for you know that you have done this for some time, and now that you have entered the years of discretion, will you now abandon the life you have lived for God? Veit[31] thinks that you have a good attitude toward God, that you are sorry to have omitted it, and that you will go to the Holy Sacrament. If you do not want to do that, because no one among us poor people on this world will <97> ever receive the Holy Sacrament worthily, then as a father to a son, I want to point out my view that whoever thinks this way is deceiving himself. You should not go to the Holy Sacrament for my sake; if you do not go because of God's love, then it is better to omit it. I do not want you to suppress your views on this. I am inclined to serve you; ask God for me that I will do this. At Hummel on Christmas Eve 1519.

3. December 21, 1520, letter from Prince John Frederick at Coburg to Spalatin.[32]

Hans Frederick, prince of Saxony.

Greetings and good wishes to my dear teacher! I have read over your letter and kindly received it; I also kindly thank you for the booklet that you dedicated to me. I kindly receive it together with the others with the gracious offer to get to know it. I have pointed out to the high-born prince, my gracious lord and father, your further offer gladly[33] to send His Grace a copy of the booklet, etc. His Grace very kindly listened to this, and graciously accepts your submissive will. I also will remember your gracious request and cling to the Gospel. Dated at Coburg on St. Thomas's Day 1520.

---

30 Handwritten, Reg. No. 806; used on pp. 41f. <30>. I reproduce this and the following writing without changing the orthography.

31 First mention of Veit Warbeck at the court of John.

32 Handwritten, without a signature, Goth. Bibl. Cod. Chart. A, 378, fol. 2; used on p. 42 <31>.

33 *gerden*, which John Frederick almost always wrote for *gern*.

4. March 24, 1525, letter from Heinrich Pomponius[34] from Gerstädt or Gera to Prince John Frederick at Weimar. For detailed reasons, he asks the prince to lift the ban on preaching from the Weimar monks.[35]

I, Heinrich Pomponius, one of the immature of our Lord Jesus Christ, am induced to write to Your Princely Grace out of true Christian love. I wish Your Princely Grace the favor and supreme kindness of Almighty God. Even though I believe without a doubt that Your Princely Grace will attribute this to me as folly and audacity, I am especially reporting about the affair of the monks at Weimar, namely, that their preaching has been suppressed by Your Princely Grace's teacher and preacher[36] at the prince's command, which I did not expect from Your Princely Grace. If this happens, Your Princely Grace must calculate what this will produce for Your Princely Grace from the common people, because the monks preach the Gospel more than all Your Princely Grace's preachers, who only out of hatred or envy have produced this prohibition and hindrance of the Gospel. I wish Your Princely <98> Grace would not so easily believe these unlearned people who have no basis in Scripture. One of them is Your Princely Grace's teacher; I partially heard some of his sermon at the castle in Weimar and wondered how Your Princely Grace could listen to this! I have also forwarded some letters to Your Princely Grace's teacher, but he has given me no answer; I will briefly point out why later. I think he is afraid or perhaps does not know how to bring anything from Scripture. It is not enough of an answer when he says that I am a fool; I certainly know that fools can speak the truth! Therefore, for the sake of God and the true Gospel, I ask that Your Princely Grace would allow the monks to preach the Gospel openly for a time. This will not count for the disadvantage of Your Princely Grace among the common people, who now say: "The princes want people to preach the Gospel, and yet they forbid the monks to do this! This happens only out of jealousy, hatred, and bickering," etc. If Your Princely Grace's teacher should try to oppose people who know or have read something, he will very soon give evidence that he should be allowed to use the crossbow.[37] Therefore, I admonish Your Princely Grace out of Christian love and faithfulness not to grant this

34 I cannot establish anything more exact about him.

35 Original, Reg. N. No. 19; used on p. 49 <38>.

36 Probably Wolfgang Stein; the prohibition of preaching occurred on March 19; Wette, 44f.

37 *auf das armbrust regen*; figure of speech? Perhaps, that he should be a soldier instead of a teacher, or that he should be cannon fodder.—Tr.

prohibition of the Gospel, which is preached in a godly and Christian way by the monks, so that Your Princely Grace and others will not be reproached like Capernaum, Chorazin, Bethsaida, and the like [Matthew 11:21–24], to whom the high grace of God's Gospel appeared, which they treated in a malicious and evil way, lest Your Princely Grace be numbered among those accursed who take offense at Christ. I ask and admonish that Your Princely Grace would not despise my writing because this admonition comes from me, a simple fellow, for Christian truth should not be despised by Christians who are baptized, even though the truth is spoken by the least creature of all; it should not be said that we have scorned good counsel because God gave it to us through unimportant people. If the Almighty God has hidden His divine wisdom from the wise and learned and revealed it to the children and the humble, why should we not receive the unquestionably divine truth of Scripture, which is brought to us by the monks in keeping with the Gospel? You should no longer desire to take away their teaching, which is so fully based on the true, divine Scriptures and has endorsed Christ Jesus through the mouth of truth.

Written on March 24, 1525, to Your Princely Grace willingly by Heinrich Pomponius, a citizen of Gera.

5. Winter 1527 letter from John Frederick to Elector John at Weimar.[38] With a detailed repetition of previous <99> discussions, he urgently asks his father once again to grant him his own household.[39]

Even though I have always been careful, as much as possible, not to trouble Your Grace with my own affairs, as I would still like to do, I am nevertheless motivated by my pressing need to ask with this letter that Your Grace would not be too busy to read this through.

And, my lord and father, the affair, as Your Grace will doubtless once again remember, is what I spoke with Your Grace about a year ago. In time past, Your Grace has had pointed out to me by the chancellor that Your Grace's feeling is that I should enter the marital estate. Now that Your Grace has carefully considered on all sides whom Your Grace would have me marry beneficially for the good of land and people, Your Grace will not hide from me that it was reported

38 The dating comes from the fact that John Frederick's nuptials were during the past year, and from his July 14, 1528, letter; see Official Document No. 7; see p. 104 <102>.

39 Draft written in his own hand, Reg. D. No. 58 II; used on pp. 38f. <27>.

to Your Grace by Count Philip of Solmes that the prince of Cleves has a daughter nearly grown of good bearing and morals, and also somewhat pretty. Then, after the marriage, so comforting and fortunate for land and people, had taken place, the Almighty God was pleased to honor the house of Saxony so that as Your Grace desires, I as the son would follow Your Grace's plan.

To give Your Grace an answer, as the chancellor has no doubt reminded Your Grace, I have given the answer among others that it is still somewhat inexpedient for me to marry. Since Your Grace would like to have me married, I would follow this plan of Your Grace out of childlike duty to my gracious lord and father. . . . But the chancellor asked me to consider how I should ask and mention to Your Grace that it is very inconvenient for me to take a wife when I do not know what I will have for my upkeep. I have nothing to hide, which I have not considered in relation to marriage, if only Your Grace would give me something of my own that I could have for my upkeep. Then I would follow Your Grace's plan that I inspect the prince of Cleves's daughter, and if she pleases me, then Your Grace would give me something of my own with which I can maintain myself at Your Grace's pleasure. Or, if Your Grace is not pleased with this, then I would propose that, if I inspect her and she pleases me, I would then venture to act, whether I receive as dowry or otherwise something in the land of Cleves or Guelph <100> with which I can support myself and my wife. However, if this is not pleasing to Your Grace, then I would ask Your Grace not to be displeased and to exempt me from taking a wife at this time. There has been all kinds of back and forth discussion about this with the chancellor and also with von Wildenfels, of which I remind Your Grace; otherwise, Your Grace has been burdened with the thought that I will seek to separate myself from Your Grace.

However, because I have existed this way for a while now, if my proposals are not pleasing to Your Grace, [I ask] that Your Grace would refrain from asking me as previously to follow Your Grace's plan that I take a wife. Von Wildenfels has pointed out to me that for the sake of Your Grace, I should follow Your Grace's plan, if Your Grace would do me this kindness with my upkeep so that my wife and I could be supported by Your Grace at court with Your Grace, then we would have no complaint about this. . . . Even though it has been very difficult for me to follow Your Grace's plan and to put my trust completely in Your Grace and to know nothing at all otherwise about my upkeep, I have nevertheless set all this aside and followed Your Grace's plan. . . . Following Your Grace's advice, my nuptials have taken place, and in every further suggestion about my upkeep from Your Grace, I have obediently followed Your Grace's pleasure.

I have reminded Your Grace of all of this and asked you to come to an understanding with me on what basis Your Grace is placing the upkeep of myself and my spouse; I wish Your Grace to consider that it is very necessary for me to know what basis is being set for my upkeep. *Your Grace could remember that you have an undivided but separate governance with your brother and when you took my mother as your wife*, you had special money for the maintenance of Your Grace's wife and Your Grace's servants. *This is very necessary for me, since I cannot do or command it myself*, so that I do not, like the young Margrave Joachim with Your Grace, have to apply to my lord and friends to sacrifice money for me.[40]

To this Your Grace has given me the innocuous answer that Your Grace is pleased, if I take a wife as Your Grace desires, to regard her, if God is willing that my wife come to our country, the same and no differently than Your Grace's sainted wife, and to regard me the same so that I will not lack anything.

When I renewed my request that Your Grace would give me the sum mentioned *for my upkeep, Your Grace answered that you would* <101> *think this over further and answer me when I have again traveled to Jülich.*

I have let this rest until several days after my return home, *and have not wanted to make any further mention of this in hope of your gracious answer.* I also have such submissive and childlike trust that I have confidently delivered over to Your Grace my dowry of 25,000 gulden, . . . so that Your Grace would all the more graciously provide my upkeep.

I have once again asked for an answer through von Wildenfels and Johann Riestel,[41] *but have only received the answer* that Your Grace provides for me and my wife in such an honorable and good way that few electors or princes provide for their sons with their wives, and that Your Grace is not going to change this. I should willingly receive with thanks what Your Grace provides.

I received this answer with not a little distress, since my request is for an independent maintenance or at least for "the sum mentioned," with which I could maintain my wife and family, etc. It was only under this assumption that I married. Second, I do not know the specifics of how other electors and princes for the most part support their sons, but I do know that some of them are supported with more than Your Grace gives to me, and that they still have to borrow to support themselves.

I once again ask Your Grace to be a gracious father to me. Your Grace's mind and heart is to be kind in these matters toward others, such as to the young margrave whose father has given him nothing; Your Grace gave money so that

40 On this loan, cf. Kius, 69.

41 Perhaps Riedesel.

His Eminence could fully maintain himself. Your Grace acted similarly with Count Heinrich von Schwarzburg at Arnstat, even though his father gave him two hundred gulden. Your Grace regarded this as right, and even pointed out to von Schwarzburg by this that he should give his son something of his own to support him. *I ask Your Grace to do the same for me*, who has obediently done everything Your Grace desires in this matter as an obedient son. *Be gracious, and do not let it happen* that I must reveal among the people that Your Grace does not give me enough to maintain myself, and accordingly must seek sacrifices of money from my lord's friends and companions. *I ask for a gracious answer.* Dated 1527.

6. Undated [winter of 1527] letter from Elector John to John Frederick in answer to No. 5. Denial of his petition.[42]

<102> *Your letter was handed over to me on Friday evening. It still does not seem proper to me to arrange* your own living *for you and your wife, nor that you should maintain your own family alongside mine. Your wife and her family have no reason to complain, for I maintain them the same way I do my second wife; you and yours also lack nothing. Your reference to me at the time of my first marriage does not fit, because I was a coruler. In the dealings with Count Günther von Schwarzburg, I was motivated by the dissension between father and son, which could easily have harmful consequences. I simply loaned the money to the young margrave under the assumption that I would get it back, without bothering myself further about the situation; as far as I am aware, they are completely different than with you. You have no cause for complaint and should be satisfied.*

7. July 14, 1528, letter from Prince John Frederick to Elector John at the same place.[43]

He reminds him of the writing submitted during the winter of the previous year about his upkeep, and renews his request for a gracious answer, so that he would not have to travel the path indicated there. Dated the Tuesday after St. Margaret's Day in 1528.[44]

---

42 Draft in Reg. D. No. 58 V; used on p. 38 <27>.

43 Handwritten draft in Reg. D. No. 58 V; used on p. 38 <27>.

44 *nach Margarethe*; St. Margaret of Antioch is honored as a saint on July 20, which fell on a Monday in 1528; this would make sense if it read *vor* instead of *nach*, or if it was dated July 21, 1528. St. Margaret of Scotland is honored as a saint on June 10. St. Margaret of Hungary is honored as a saint on January 18. St. Margaret of England is honored as a saint on February 3.—Tr.

8. Some thoughts about the Diet of Speyer, especially about the king, undated [from Weimar, ca. February 25,[45] 1529]. Explanation of the reasons why Ferdinand should not be chosen as Roman king. Discussion of the way Saxony should proceed at the diet to prevent his election.[46]

In God's name. Amen.

The first point to be considered is that at the upcoming diet, the chief thing they will attempt to accomplish will be the election of King Ferdinand of Hungary and Bohemia, Archduke of Austria, to be Roman king, in relation to this, it is to be considered that if this event takes place—may the warm-hearted God graciously prevent it!—then the holy empire will be completely deprived of its free election, and the freedom that the holy empire and especially the German nation have previously had will be turned into an eternal bondage and hereditary empire.

It is easy to imagine that, after the house of Austria has now had the government of the empire for nearly a century, if <103> Austria is allowed to have this always as long as the ruling family lasts, this will, humanly speaking, result in difficulties and unrest. In addition to how tyrannically they have attempted to act toward the estates of the holy empire, as is shown daily, what they now are doing with the kingdoms of Hungary and Bohemia, as also in the hereditary lands, easily reveals what will happen in the future in the empire. There are many other reasons evident, which it is inconvenient to relate.

Accordingly, it is highly necessary for the electors carefully to carry out the duties they owe to the holy empire not to give up this attempt.

In addition to all this, it is very important to realize that through King Ferdinand, they will attempt, as is already the case in his hereditary lands, to force everyone in any estate to believe and regard as Christian whatever pleases him, whether it was invented by him or by the pope or by the devil. How much this should move each person in his conscience, each person's conscience will, God willing, teach him.[47]

This may be obtained from the electors and princes if, instead of the

---

45 This was sent with a February 26, 1529, letter from Weimar to John (Loc. 10671 "Concerning the Election of King Ferdinand," 1531, fol. 25f. handwritten).

46 Draft in his own hand; Loc. 10671 "Concerning the Election of King Ferdinand," 1531. Copies ibid., and in the same place, "Schreiben und Bedenken," fol. 41–48. There is some confusion in the copies, since the pages of the draft have fallen into disorder. I am essentially following the draft, which certainly also is not without obscurities; used on pp. 51f. <42>, 74f. <69>

47 The copies mistakenly conclude the whole document here.

common good of the Holy Roman Empire, they regard their own good higher. Yet we hope that God will not let the electors and princes fall so far that they do not prevent action being taken on behalf of the king. They should point out to the common estates and especially to the cities and those in them that the freedom of the empire will be made into the king's inheritance. They should further point out to the cities that in such an election, only a true Turk will be elected, for the Turk could not persecute the Christian believers and the Word of God more or deal more tyrannically with the Christian believers than this king is ready to do.

It is easy to judge how much this election concerns the divine Word and those who cling to it. Although God has obviously commanded and wants obedience to be shown to every government as far as body and goods are concerned, he does not yet have authority over those who are in the empire; yet if he is elected, and this is not prevented by God's help, then he will be the government of the empire.

Each one should consider, before it hits home, how difficult it will be to have a tyrant and persecutor of the divine Word as his lord, <104> for if he becomes king, then nothing else can be done against him.

God's Word is clear: "Be subject to the government" [Romans 13:1], whether it is evil or good. If we want to be Christians and praise Christ's words, then we must tolerate from him all persecution because of the divine Word and otherwise all temporal tyranny. *Now, if we are seeking ways to resist this ruthless tyrant of body and soul, we must first ask God* to grant us grace, wisdom, and strength to resist this tyrant and persecutor of the divine Word as our lord, and then each one who clings to the divine Word can sacrifice his body and goods and everything to resist this tyrant. For who would not say before God and the world that it would be more Christian, more honorable, and better to be slain and perish in this Christian work than by the Turk? The Turk desires only external dominion over body and goods, but this ruthless tyrant desires to give souls to the devil and use the goods for his own pleasure.

Each one should take this to heart. Once he is elected, our effort and work are lost. The representatives of the cities should understand this no differently than confidentially, but also Christian and well-meant, and consider what they ought to do for themselves, their wives and children, and for the commoners, and let their thoughts be known.

If the princes, counts, and knights who cling to the divine Word are willing to resist, and there is no other way to prevent this election, then they can hope that God will send other ways and means in which they can faithfully sacrifice their bodies and goods to prevent this.

May God grant His grace so that people do not become afraid and think, "If I do these things and he becomes king, how fiercely he will punish me for what I did against him!"

They should consider more what they are bound before God and the world to do. Even if the other electors and princes do not consider their honor and loyalty, oath and duty to the empire, this should not be neglected by those who understand and know what irreparable damage will result from this for the empire; they should work diligently, no matter what happens.

Second, whether or not he becomes king, if he can banish and expel all who adhere to the divine Word from the country, he will certainly do so, since they are very violent; therefore, I hope that I have done enough that people need not fear.

<105> If this effort is pursued in every way with the electors, princes, and common estates, each according to his confession, as it is considered valuable, I have no doubt that if effort is diligently applied while asking for God's grace, it will happen that Ferdinand is elected king by none of those who hold to the divine Word. If there are none, this is the will of the almighty God, to whom this and all other matters are entrusted to His divine will, who does this for His honor and glory. Amen.

Thoughts on why in the present situation and the way things are everywhere in the empire, it is not good to have a Roman king:

First, it is to be considered that the imperial majesty as the true lord can in no way be advised to have a Roman king as a coruler,[48] for these reasons, that it is impossible for two lords to rule side by side, and it is just as impossible for the subject estates of the empire to be able to serve two lords at the same time and to observe their commands and prohibitions at the same time.

If this is to be agreed on, it can happen in no other way than that the imperial majesty completely relinquishes to the Roman king all jurisdiction in the holy empire together with all his glory and subsequently takes no interest at all in the empire, but lets the king do whatever he wants in the empire.

If this is to happen, then the imperial majesty will no longer be honored in the empire, but will be considered by the allies of the empire more as the king of Spain than as the Roman emperor, which will have the result that the imperial majesty will be relieved of all imperial honor. However, after it was included in the announcement of this diet that they should speak about

48 Note in the margin of the draft: "It is also to be considered that if the imperial majesty has a son and would bequeath the imperial election to him, it is a concern that the imperial honor would never stop coming to his majesty's lineage that would come from him."

a general or national free Christian council, since no council can be held,[49] whether it is general or national, unless the Roman emperor is present, it would not be amiss to delay the election of the Roman king until the end of the council, so that when his imperial majesty arrives, a way can be found for his majesty to be in the empire and rule it.

This also should not happen for many significant reasons; at the present time, there is danger in the election of a Roman king, especially because of how often in the election of a Roman king schism has arisen between the electors and <106> the princes, so that often two kings have been elected at the same time, and each has separate adherents from the electors, princes, and estates of the empire, from which have arisen dissension, war, shedding of blood, and all misery in the empire.

Because this often happened in previous times among our ancestors, in these anxious times, it will be much greater when it happens. It is especially to be considered how much at the present time the common man is inclined to rebellion against the government, and how easily such rebellion can be expected because of a troublesome election. In addition, it is well-known that almost all electors, princes, and the common estates of the empire are completely divided on the Word of God and faith, so that each side expects nothing from the other; whichever party gets a Roman king for its own advantage will try to exterminate the other side. It can easily be grasped from this that neither party can tolerate someone from the opposite party becoming king, and before they would tolerate this, they would put their lives and goods at risk. From this, nothing else is to be considered but that more shedding of blood will happen in the empire than has been heard of before.

A further motivating factor is the concern about the Turks, especially if they become aware of the discord in the empire; may the almighty God graciously prevent this!

We must consider what can further come from this, lest all Germany go to ruin, which is in God's hands.[50]

We should further consider that if a king is elected who is against one of the parties in the empire, that party may join with the common peasants and elect their own opposition king who is suitable to them, in whom they think they can find protection—whether it is France, England, or even the Turk. Therefore, it is very necessary to consider all of this that might happen and

---

49 In the margin of the draft: "in the German nation."

50 Read *da for got sei* instead of *da got for sei*.—Tr.

especially refrain from electing a king because of these and other excellent reasons. Rather, we should diligently and submissively petition the imperial majesty through embassies and otherwise so that, considering the difficulties that are daily expected to arise in the Holy Roman Empire, His Majesty would himself come into the empire, investigate this, etc. Without this, it will be impossible to oppose the Turks and maintain peace and justice in the empire.[51]

Accordingly, because of many reasons that concern the eternal and temporal welfare of the holy empire, high necessity <107> demands that the almighty God be asked to prevent such things . . . and that we agree on such human ways and means, for if we have the patience,[52] God will grant the increase.

It is first to be considered that when arriving at the diet, the electors diligently meet alone with their councilors or messengers and faithfully confer according to their duties about the matter of a Roman king, which the imperial majesty will attempt through his orator, and learn what each is inclined to do; we should work diligently so that all the electors can unanimously give the imperial majesty a negative answer about the king.

In this or another way, it is to be considered that the electors have elected the imperial majesty out of submissiveness according to the duties they owe the empire to be emperor and lord of themselves and the whole Roman Empire; since they have and keep him as their majesty, there is no need for any other lord or king; they would not like to have any other as their lord, emperor, and king except the imperial majesty; they are confident that the imperial majesty will be and remain their only emperor and lord, and since they have desired the imperial majesty alone for their lord, they will take a chance on no other lord or king than they have. In consideration of the duty Your Majesty has to be our capable lord and emperor, Your Majesty was elected free of all duty except the current difficulties to be Roman king and emperor in submissive confidence that Your Imperial Majesty will be and remain with them and the other imperial estates of the holy empire as their only emperor and lord. Because of the other estates, the electors have petitioned and asked Your Majesty graciously to spare the electors the danger of having to elect your brother to be Roman king, because this would be against the duty they owe to the empire. May Your Majesty arrange and proceed to rule in your own person in the holy empire, and be the most gracious emperor and lord of the electors and their princes and imperial estates. This would remove the difficult problems that

---

51 Here the copies break off; the rest is only in the draft.

52 *erwait* (*erwählt?*)—Tr.

exist everywhere in the empire and establish and preserve peace and justice, discipline and order in the empire. It would show Your Imperial Majesty's office given to you by God at your birth if you granted what the electors are seeking. . . . The answer that belongs to this should be considered further.

Now, if the orator is satisfied with what the imperial majesty did, then he had his way; if not, then let him act so that the electors are bound to one another, so that no one <108> would refuse answer to another in any business, and so that all business and answers would be handled in the same way.

If, then, the spokesman harps further on the imperial majesty's pledge that his brother will be elected Roman king and proves this with all kinds of reasons, he should repeat the first answer and point out that the electors had no doubt that if the imperial majesty heard their answer, he would be pleased with it; especially with regard to their duties, they would like to have Your Imperial Majesty with them as their true, natural lord and benefit from him, and so submissively cling to the imperial majesty with body and property. The electors would not conceal from the spokesman that their duty also involves the Golden Bull, that when there is an election of a Roman king, they promise to elect no one except the one they consider in their conscience most beneficial to the governance of the holy empire. Accordingly, the imperial majesty should not insist that the electors carry out their duty toward the Golden Bull,[53] and the imperial majesty should consider that because of the information reported to the imperial majesty, they will further insist that the imperial majesty carry out his duties, which he owes the empire in this business, so that they would never do harm to the imperial majesty.

Accordingly, the electors want the spokesman to be favorable as he reports this finally to His Majesty and submissively ask Your Majesty for your own sake to spare the electors further consideration of your duties, to overlook your constant desire for a Roman king, and give attention to what is most important to the electors, who would like to see Your Majesty as their lord, emperor, and king in the empire. However, if this is not pleasing to Your Imperial Majesty and you want to have a king in the empire, they ask that the imperial majesty would let the electors have an election day in keeping with the Golden Bull of Emperor Charles IV, when without constraint they can, according to their duties, elect whomever each one in his conscience thinks will be the Roman king most beneficial in his rule for the holy empire and for whom they can answer before God. The electors will, with God's help, demonstrate this in

---

53 In the margin: "Note the order that the imperial majesty gave to examine what was printed."

their election, as it is proper for them to do according to their duties as faithful electors.

Now, whoever the spokesman thinks is best to report this to the imperial majesty in his own person, *the electors will be satisfied. If, however, it was inconvenient for the spokesman to do this, then the electors would think it best to send their own ambassadors to the imperial majesty and to report this and whatever else is necessary to the imperial majesty.*

<109> *If they achieved unanimity among the electors about this, then it would be enough for this time that Ferdinand was not elected as Roman king.*

If, however, they observe that the electors in part or all of them will not persist on this path, but are deceived *by Ferdinand to elect him king, then they should proceed against this in the following way*: Some princes who can be trusted should be notified confidentially, such as Margrave George of Brandenburg, Prince Philip, Prince Ernst of Brunswick, Prince Heinrich of Mecklenburg, the landgrave, and the bishops of Osnabrück and Anhalt. It is to be expected that the Palatinate is opposed to such an election, and the Palatinate can point this out to some princes who might be at the diet, such as Prince Wilhelm and Prince Ludwig of Bavaria, Prince Friedrich of Bavaria, Prince Otto Heinrich of Bavaria, some bishops who were his brothers, such as the bishop of Speyer, the bishop of Regensburg, the bishop of Freisingen, the bishop of Worms, etc. Then the secular princes can in his presence alone call for councilors or ambassadors, and the clergy similarly can call for other spiritual princes, especially for councilors and ambassadors, and each group point this out to their own kind, the clergy to clergy, the secular to secular, and they will likely reach the point according to the old praiseworthy custom, *by laying a common basis among some electors, a Roman king would be chosen without a free election, and the house of Austria remain hereditary lord of the empire. After they learned this with dread, they could not neglect to point this out, in the hope that they are ready to join them in preventing it. If it comes down to these princes having doubts about this, then they should apply their counsel to this: Since this above all depends on the electors, some of the oldest and most capable princes should be sent to point out to the electors how this concerns them. They should, then, put this burden on them and explain that in their right to vote, they should not be restricted, but should remember the stipulations of the Golden Bull. If they were to infringe on these, the princes would have to see to it that harm was averted. They hoped, however, that it would not come to this and that they would act properly* and[54] according to their duties. They hoped they would look at nothing as a threat or a burden, or at any promise to give them

54 From here on also in the copies; see p. 105 <103>.

many great things, or at anything else. They would sacrifice themselves if they thought that would not cause them trouble, so that they would not forsake them like the electors who truly mean well for the Roman Empire with the sacrifice <110> of body and goods, but would faithfully remain with them.

If they would furnish this, then they would observe what has been pointed out no differently than because it achieves what they cannot omit according to their duties; they would do this to provide for them as for their friends; they would consider what would benefit the empire, and accordingly show that they will grant the electors nothing detrimental to the empire and which causes endless difficulty; along with what they ought to do for God and the world, they will as much as they can always be obliging.

Now, there is no doubt that if this proposal is made to the electors, it will please the other princes who love the freedom of the empire and who hope to God that this will succeed in Ferdinand not becoming king. May God grant us His grace for this! Amen.

••

9. March 13, 1529, letter from Prince John Frederick in Weimar to Count Wilhelm von Neuenahr. John's journey to the diet; summons to come there and give secret reports to Minkwitz. The elector of Cologne. Reasons why John Frederick is remaining at home. Concerns about Geldern. The interrupted journey to Bohemia. The libels authored by Prince George and Luther. The possible journey of the emperor into the kingdom, and the planned election of the Roman king. Neuenahr's service with King Ferdinand. [Answer to the January 31, 1529, letter from the count. Cornelius 10:153–55.][55]

Thanks for the good wishes. I and my spouse had expected your previous writing after your visit.

Thanks for the offer to come to the diet if I am going there. You will already know that my father has in the meantime arrived at the diet. His Grace has taken with him as intimate councilors Count Albrecht von Mansfeld, Hans von Minkwitz, and Dr. Brück, His Grace's old chancellor. Accordingly, I ask you to let nothing prevent you from traveling there quickly to tell His Grace what you regard to be necessary, and to tell His Grace what will especially please him. However, what you want to tell me do not write down, but report it privately to Hans von Minkwitz who can repeat it to me.

---

55 Draft in his own hand (Reg. E. fol. 37a, No. 83, Bl. 210–12); used on pp. 57 <48>, 73 <68>.

After I observed in your previous writing that my dear lord and friend, the elector of Cologne, is a good Saxon, and I have never found him different, I think it would be a very good thing for you to do on the way <111> to arrange for him and my gracious lord and father to have an especially friendly confession and time for intimate conversation. This could accomplish much good, and as far as I can foresee, my gracious lord and father would not lack anything for this.

I also desire that you graciously greet my lord of Cologne for me and wish him a happy, Christian condition for his soul and body; it would give me special joy if he would experience this.

I am remaining at home at this time because of the spread of oppression, so that there is someone in the land; if that were not necessary, I would much rather like to be at the diet than not, for it is my opinion that there will be rather unusual glorious unions, which have recently been heard of.

I am happy to hear that those from Brabant and the lord of Geldern are united, if only it lasts, but I am concerned that they will not stay on the way to peace. However, if something detrimental should arise from my lord of Cologne, my lord father, and the prince of Cleves and Jülich, who are loyal to me, I know what to advise to help change this, and I would ask that it be done in a kind and loyal way.

Hans von Minkwitz can tell you what is necessary about why I again returned from receiving a fief from the king of Bohemia for my gracious lord and father and other princes of Saxony, and what the situation is between the house of Saxony and the Bohemians.

I am somewhat surprised that the libels of my cousin Prince George and of Luther, which they wrote against each other, have reached you, for I did not think either writing was worth that much that they would spread that far, for there is little good to be found in either; they would have been much better not written than written, which is hard to prevent; Luther has been commanded by my gracious lord and father to stop writing on this matter.

I am delighted that the imperial majesty will come this summer from Spain to Germany; for many reasons, no greater benefit could happen to the empire than that we Germans would have our true emperor and lord with us. I am greatly concerned, however, about the rumor that is spreading in the land that the imperial majesty will dissolve the empire and the one from Waldkirch will have the command especially to deal with the electors all together on behalf of the imperial majesty, and that Your Majesty's brother, King Ferdinand, will be made Roman king. Some say that this is mostly why this diet was announced,

<112> so that now it is hard to imagine that the imperial majesty will come into the kingdom.

As far as your service to King Ferdinand is concerned, I have written you nothing else than my opinion, and have had Altenburg point out my feelings about this; I will be satisfied with that, for you will know to do what you consider best. I must write to you from a full heart, however, that I hope that when King Ferdinand becomes Roman king and you become his steward, that I will still benefit from your old loyalty, so that I will not have to stand outside, but you will help me to have an audience quickly.

You can let me know whatever else you know about the king's ways. Dated in Weimar on the Saturday after Laetare in 1529.

10. March 22, 1529, letter from Prince John Frederick in Weimar to Hans von Minkwitz. Eating meat and preaching at the diet. The councilors should see to it that the elector remains firm. Hans v. d. Planitz should not accept all the orders of the king for the elector. Franz von Lüneburg. Prince George's answer to Minkwitz. Thoughts about the election of the king. Prince George is not coming to the diet, nor is the elector of Brandenburg. Orders for Taubenheim and Planitz.[56]

Thanks for your detailed report; I cannot answer all the articles. Joy that all arrived healthy in Speyer.

I am not surprised that the king emphasizes eating meat and preaching so much, for I think the devil is forcefully riding on him and his servants in this matter; the devil thinks that if preaching is allowed at this diet, as I hope to God it will be, then it might introduce a limitation that people will have to tolerate at this diet.

I hope, however, that you and the other councilors of my gracious lord will not advise him differently than that His Grace stand firm on the divine Word, no matter what happens, for I know that my gracious lord will not abandon that, even if he is advised differently with beautiful words, as can happen, but which I do not at all expect from all you councilors.

I also think it would be good to restrain Hans von der Planitz, so that he refrains from proposing these things about the king to my gracious lord and father, lest he use the excuse that he is my gracious lord's servant who is exempt

56 Handwritten, Reg. E. fol. 37a, No. 83, fol. 63–65, handwritten copy, ibid., fol 215–17; used on p. 76 <71>.

from the royal majesty and can act on His Grace through other servants and councilors of his royal majesty; I think all such attempts should be omitted.

<113> *Prince Franz von Lüneburg is not coming to the diet. The chancellor of Lüneburg will inform you of the reasons for this by word of mouth*, no matter how good those reasons are.

I am not at all pleased that Prince George gave you such a useless answer; it did no harm, however, when you forwarded this to the king as the true liege lord and asked his royal majesty's advice. As far as my thoughts are concerned, I would like to hear the advice that something good can be accomplished by this if God grants His grace for it. But it would be a good idea for you councilors to write against doing nothing else than writing libels against each other, which only wastes time and overloads the matter. This is why we have to wait until my thoughts come up again; I know well the tricks of the doctors; God grant that these are omitted! I have again replied[57] to the writing of my gracious lord and father with my own hand regarding this matter, as was doubtless shown to you, and I have no doubt that you will do your utmost, as much as you can, so that we do not get this man as our lord. Count Albrecht will now have arrived, to whom my thoughts should be read, so that nothing is neglected, for I think it is time to take up these matters with the electors, for we can easily wait too long. . . . Dated in Weimar on the Monday after Palm Sunday in 1529.

[P.S. fol. 64] my cousin Prince George wanted to be at the diet in person, but his beloved whom he wanted to have with him became sick, and so he sent Hans von Schonberg and Doctor Werter. So the margrave cannot get away from the prostitute in the armory,[58] but, according to my information, will appoint the bishop of Lebus to do that.

Greet Christoph von Taubenheim, and apologize for me that I have not written back to him. Hans should also greet the black noble for me, and tell him to avoid the foolish things connected with the king, or when I come, I will throw him into the water!

Provide me with two large leather bottles covered with pitch.

---

57 On March 22 (handwritten in Reg. E. fol. 37a, No. 83, fol. 61) without any significant new information.

58 This refers to the relationship of Joachim with Mrs. Hornung.

11. March 26, 1529, letter from Prince John Frederick in Weimar to Elector John. Answer to John's letter on the seventeenth, the content of which is almost completely reflected in this letter. Suspicion that the articles on help against the Turks and on the government have been returned to Ferdinand. Admonition to oppose the repeal of the previous imperial departure instructions.[59]

<114> I have read Your Grace's writing and . . . since the diet has begun, I am glad to hear that God has granted that things were handled beneficially for the praise of God and the welfare of the empire. However, the articles that the imperial majesty had shown to the estates of the empire were somewhat severe, and it can certainly be concluded from this that they mostly came from the king of Bohemia. It is my opinion that the king sent these articles to the imperial majesty, who then circulated them, or that the king as governor in the holy empire made them more severe and had them read, for the imperial majesty had commanded the same thing from Spain. It is easy to conclude from this that these two articles about help against the Turks and the maintenance of the government and the supreme court benefit no one except only the king. The Turk teaches him most harshly, because his royal majesty must cover the overdraft, which must be obtained from the government of his hereditary lands, which will then be rolled onto the estates of the empire.

It is frightening to hear from Your Grace's writing that the departure instructions from Speyer set up on the basis of previous diets by the electors, princes, and estates, in which King Ferdinand as governor for his imperial majesty, together with the appointed princes who were also commissioners, agreed, are now at this diet completely defunct and reversed. It is easy to figure out from this what people have in mind! If God is willing, this will not be granted by most who stand with Your Grace (to speak the way the world does), and Your Grace must hold with those who adhere to the divine Word, and especially with the estates. If Your Grace holds firm, draws the others to yourself, and does not let them turn aside, then with God's grace, the previous departure instructions will be preserved, especially if Your Grace anticipates the resolution.[60]

Since Your Grace has sent me a sword to make me useful, which pleases me,

---

59 Handwritten, Reg. E. fol. 37a, No. 83, Bl. 69f.; handwritten copy, ibid., Bl. 217–19; used on pp. 52 <42>, 75f. <70>, 77 <72>.

60 In the draft, there is a section in which it is recommended that the question of faith be taken up before the question of help for the Turks, in order to make Ferdinand more yielding on the first question.

I will seek in turn submissively to gain merit with Your Grace as my gracious lord and father.

I know of no special news to tell Your Grace, except that on Palm Sunday, Your Grace's faithful old servant, Markus Schart, died at Gessen (?). . . . Dated at Weimar very quickly on Good Friday 1529.

12. April 8, 1529, letter from Prince John Frederick at Weimar to Elector John. Answer to his March 30 letter. <115> Explanation that Saxony must take the lead in the election question, even if this does not achieve anything with the electors. Advice to begin with the Palatinate, Trier, and Cologne. If these cannot be gained, then they must follow the other paths recommended earlier. P.S. Some thoughts about help against the Turks are sent to Anhalt, Mansfeld, and Minkwitz.[61]

I have received the letter Your Grace wrote back with your own hand about these matters, dated at Speyer on the Tuesday after Easter, which I received on the Monday after Quasimodogeniti. . . . I am especially joyful that Your Grace received my thoughts with fatherly pleasure, and I have no doubt at all that Your Grace will know how to act in consideration of the welfare of the empire and without reproach. But I also note from Your Grace's writing that nothing has yet been done about this. Now I want to remind Your Grace to give attention in your further reflections that nothing is reported except what has been approved by the other electors, lest everything Your Grace intends becomes more difficult to carry out. Before Your Grace consults with the electors about these things, Your Grace could add in my foolish thoughts so that Your Grace does not suspect anyone, for the following reasons:

Your Grace had pointed out to the electors what kind of an attempt was made on Your Grace by the imperial majesty's spokesman von Hildesheim or Waldkirch because of the imperial majesty regarding what should be done to His Majesty's brother in this affair. Your Grace should not doubt that such an attempt would have succeeded if Your Grace had not pointed this out. Moreover, Your Grace regards this to be an important matter, because he and Your Grace will be together and can confer with each other, so that if there is a further attempt, each will know what you have conferred about and what

61 Handwritten, Reg. E. fol. 37a, No. 83, Bl. 228–30; handwritten draft from April 6 in Loc. 10671 "Schreiben und Bedenken," fol. 31f.; used on p. 77 <72>.

answer is to be given to please each elector, and you can unite and agree on equality in these matters.

No one can hold against Your Grace this and similar information that Your Grace considers, but rather should praise Your Grace for faithfully keeping in mind the welfare of the empire. However, if Your Grace does not think it good to speak with all the electors at the same time about these things Your Grace is thinking about, then Your Grace has good reasons <116> to encourage Trier and the Palatinate, after the diet was held in Fulda or Gelnhausen,[62] that the two electors and Your Grace should come together and confer about these things, even though the Palatinate revoked that diet with its codicil. As much as I have been reminded by Your Grace, he and Your Grace and the bishop of Trier should confer at the diet about these things, so that Your Grace would have sufficient opportunity to speak privately with the two electors about these things.

It is my opinion that because Count Wilhelm von Neuenahr is at Speyer, Your Grace should speak in private with your councilor and servant, for he will keep this and other matters completely secret, especially what von Neuenahr learns from the elector of Cologne about his thoughts and inclinations. Now, Your Grace will find from what von Neuenahr does that Your Grace can complete matters with Cologne or not; it is my opinion that Your Grace will find nothing else in my lord of Cologne than that he is favorably inclined to the divine Word for a bishop and intends all kindness with Your Grace.

Now, if Your Grace with divine help finds this business with the three electors to be upright, and that they agree unanimously with Your Grace on a Christian and honorable answer, then Your Grace will, humanly speaking, have anticipated everything that can arise from this business.

However, if Your Grace finds things different, which may God graciously prevent, then Your Grace can proceed in the other way, and Your Grace can carefully carry this out with a submissive mind in all kindness and faithfulness, which Your Grace will understand as faithfully as I mean it. . . . Dated at Weimar on the Thursday after Quasimodogeniti in 1529.

In the original on Bl. 229 there is a P.S.

. . . Since Your Grace has written to me about aid against the Turks, I will not conceal from Your Grace that I have carefully put down some thoughts about aid against the Turks only as an aid to the memory. I have sent this for further consideration to my uncle von Anhalt, Count Albrecht von Mansfeld,

62 Is this a reference to the negotiations in 1525/26?

and Hans von Minkwitz, because I did not think it worth troubling Your Grace with. However, if Your Grace finds from the above named uncle von Anhalt and the others that there is something in this worth troubling Your Grace with, then Your Grace can demand it from them.

. . . Dated as above.

<117> 13. April 14, 1529, letter from Prince John Frederick in Weimar to Princess Elisabeth of Saxony. Explanation of why he writes so seldom. The controversy between Prince George and Luther. The league and the departure instructions from Dessau. Pack. George's unfounded complaints. Rejection of the allegation that he caused Landgrave Philip to cling to Pack and, in general, dangerously influenced the landgrave. It is not John's fault but George's fault that George and Elector John have not reconciled. The effects of the Evangelical preachers on the diet.[63]

If I have not written to you for a long time, this has not happened, as you think, because I am angry with you, but it is, as I previously pointed out to you, because of the cares I always write about. So you see how seldom I greet you with letters, and I cannot know whom I can trust to deliver the letters, for at the present time, trust is very dangerous, since money can turn people into scoundrels. For this and no other reason, I have stopped writing to you. If, however, you still want me to write to you, whether the letters get into other hands or not, and you have no disadvantage from this—this is not a simple matter, for if someone else sees what I write, I am a little hesitant about this, even if it were otherwise good.

But you wrote me about Dr. Luther's writing against my dear cousin, Prince George of Saxony. I can truthfully write you that I am not pleased with either writing against the other and must tolerate this on both sides. However, as far as what my gracious lord and father is obliged to do in this, he has often been asked not to rebuke Luther and has given the same answer, with which he had to be satisfied. You doubtless know enough about the attempt and the answer, and so I will not trouble you with further news about this.

Regarding what I have written to you about the league, I can (God be praised!) remember what you learned, especially that it depends on the departure instructions from Dessau. I certainly know that my dear cousin,

63 Handwritten draft, Reg. A. 240; used on pp. 57 <48>, 63 <54>, 72f. <67>.

Prince George, has held my gracious lord and father to these Dessau departure instructions at the Diet of Naumburg. They were put into writing, and they united about them, even though there was little peace in them.

We still have the writing the imperial majesty sent from Spain to the two counts, Count Wilhelm von Nassau <118> and Count Ebharten von Königstein, in which the imperial majesty points out how and from whom it has been reported about the league some electors have undertaken, namely the cardinal and archbishop of Mainz and Magdeburg; Prince George of Saxony; Prince Heinrich of Brunswick; and some other electors, princes, and estates of the empire to prevent the Lutherans from undertaking to compel anyone to their unbelief through tricks or force. They have formed a league with one another, etc., to investigate and learn all kinds of things. This is not incredible, because the imperial majesty has brought along a writing that reports something about this.

However, I will have nothing to do with what Pack has said about the league, which you have heard from Wittenberg, Count Albrecht von Mansfeld, and me. What he told you needs no vindication, for what he said publicly before all the princes who were at Cassel sufficiently shows that he has reported false and unfounded things.

Regarding what my dear cousin, Prince George, has complained to you about, which he could never attain from my gracious lord and father, that His Grace has written about what will happen with Pack, I will not leave you uninformed that I remember he made an attempt with my gracious lord and father, to which His Grace always answered that, God willing, he would remain incorruptible by human partiality. You can have the same answer if you ask your own father, which would not be unreasonable.

However, since he tries to drag me in so that I do not find fault with this, I can truthfully write you that if he ever writes or requests that from me, I will not give him any answer. Because I and Count Albrecht have to bear the cross that all the guilt is ours, I am glad to hear that you have such good people around you to impose this injustice on us. But I know that the count and I and the other councilors of my gracious lord and father advise nothing else than we are obliged to by our relationship to you, which is nothing other than Christian, honorable, and fully justified. But I do believe that I would be a more devout cousin and the others faithful advisors if we were to advise my gracious lord and father to do everything that pleases my dear cousin. Therefore, without regard for God or conscience, we would completely become his servants, and whatever he would have us advise, my gracious lord and father must do.

<119> But if any of your advisors would impose something different on us, I kindly ask you to tell them not to speak to you without us, since we are responsible for it. If, God willing, our answer is heard, then those who have made this up will have to be ashamed.

You point out that you have been told that it is my fault that your brother held so firmly to Pack, etc. I must tolerate what devout people impose on me against you and otherwise, for I do not know who is spreading this stuff. If you would name them to me, I could talk with them, and you could see what is true and what is false.

I can truthfully write to you that my dear brother, the landgrave, has not spoken with me for a long time. I can tolerate what you and everyone accuse me of advising him, for I have not advised him anything dishonorable, in spite of the accusations, but only that he would answer honorably and justly.

Since you feel that you have to point out to me somewhat harshly that you only have one brother, and it is being spread among the people that he was misled, etc., I will not hide from you that I was not a little troubled that you would turn on me without hearing my answer, as if I misled your brother, for I had hoped to God that you knew me well enough that I am more opposed than devoted to things that are dishonorable. Much less would I mislead anyone into dishonorable things, for I trust in God that I have done well and cannot justly be accused of this. Although I know you can only write what you have been told, I think I should be spared from this. You think that I am burdened with your brother's misfortune, but I do not like to see it any more than you or anyone else. I would do as much as I could to prevent him being misled, which you and he were very concerned about, for I know (God be praised!) that I am free of the guilt of advising him wrongly; if I had been in his place, I would have done the same and helped him.

But since you point out how your father would like to be very friendly and get along with my gracious lord and father and holds that out to us, I will report to you that my gracious lord and father has always sought nothing else and still seeks nothing else than that he would like from the heart to get along with your father and that he would know that my dear father expects to get along together with him, which your <120> father will not do. So that you can have a further report on these matters, I am forwarding to you the answer my gracious lord and father gave to his cousin's province that they sought about the business of that province,[64] from which you can find who is proposing this to

64 Cf. Burkhardt, *Landtagsakten*, 1:188f.

the other, for my gracious lord and father will propose, as the Wends propose to the Germans that the Germans retain the owl and the Wends retain the rabbit, or the Wends would retain the rabbit and the Germans would let the owl go. This is the way people deal with him and say that he will not accept what is proposed to him, but if we for our part should have the rabbit, we would say, "Get along by listening to the owl."

I would like to be with you no less than you write, and converse about these things.

Regarding the news you desire to hear, I know of nothing to write except that my gracious lord and father is vigorous and healthy with his people at the Diet of Speyer, and although they tried to prevent him from eating meat during the fast and to prevent the preachers of the divine Word, he has retained them with divine help, and six or eight thousand people went to the preacher of my father and my brother the landgrave, since he preached twice a day. . . . May God grant you knowledge of His divine Word and preserve you in it. Dated in Weimar on the *Wednesday after Misericordias Domini in 1529.*

14. April 14, 1529, letter from Count Albrecht von Mansfeld [in Speyer] to Prince John Frederick. Regret that he is not at the diet. Report on the negotiations conducted with Trier and Cologne on the question of electing the king, with no hope for the Palatinate. The Cologne-Jülich controversy.[65]

Your Princely Grace will have learned from Hans von Minkwitz what has been discussed so far; the chancellor will also send Your Grace a transcript of all the proceedings.

In my estimation, there will be no diet at which Your Princely Grace needs to be present more than this one; the business has been partially reported to Your Princely Grace, but the reasons cannot be shared in writing.

I conversed with the bishop of Trier for almost an hour on the business of a Roman king. His Electoral Grace graciously listened to my report that I had found him a verbose man. Although I informed him of the circumstances, it finally came down to his agreement to converse with Your Princely Grace's father. His Electoral Grace's heart was not in agreement with the man, <121> but there is great fear that the man who would like to be king is an adherent of the supposed clergy, etc. In the discussions my gracious lord had with him on other matters, I would hope it would bear fruit, but it is possible that they will

65 Handwritten, Reg. E. fol. 37a, No. 83, Bl. 89–92; used on p. 76 <71>.

not get along. This is how things stand with Cologne, for the count of Moers,[66] the bishop's brother, the [count of] Manderstadt, together with Hans and myself reached an opinion that the bishop cannot share for his chapter and region, so it was only a friendly conversation. Accordingly, Hans and I had a short list on which we conferred orally, together with the two lords who would forward it to the bishop; however, there was no final answer about whether the bishop agrees with this, since it depends on the bishop taking the field and conferring with my lord, the elector of Saxony, when it pleases His Electoral Grace. I spoke with my lord yesterday about this and will again, and then will send to Your Princely Grace a list of the notes forwarded to both counts in this matter.

I have not dealt with the Palatinate, since he knows no Saxon, but this can happen with gaps, which will not be omitted. I will investigate this and not withhold it from Your Princely Grace; I will work at this as much as it depends on me. We have dealt with both electors of Trier and Cologne, but not with Cologne separately.

I will apply myself in everything as much as possible for the welfare and pleasure of Your Princely Grace, not sparing body and property. I have no doubt that Your Princely Grace will continue to be my gracious lord, for I will not merit more in these matters, etc. *Private matters*. Dated in haste by my hand on April 14, 1529.

[*note fol. 90*]. It is understood from the conversation that was held, that the two electors of Cologne and Saxony cannot remain afoul of each other but, as far as a Roman king is concerned, must agree and stand as one person.

In case the councilors and provinces of Cologne and Jülich do not find a solution to their dispute, the elector of Saxony will seek to authorize friendly discussions; if the action His Electoral Grace seeks through Cologne is accepted by Jülich, discussions will take place; if His Electoral Grace is prevented from doing this in his own person, it will happen through His Electoral Grace's son.

---

66 That is, John I, died 1533.

15. April 26, 1529, letter from Prince John Frederick in Weimar to Hans von Minkwitz. Complaint about his laziness in writing letters.[67]

Thanks for your letter. My father wrote to report on the business of the Gospel. Although I <122> had learned this before on my own, he also wrote it to me.

I write many letters to the count of Anhalt, Count Albrecht, and you, but receive few answers. I do not know from this whether the letters do not reach you or whether you are drinking too much in the evening so that you cannot write! No letter has again come from you. The count of Anhalt has written me nothing in three weeks.

Financial concerns. John Frederick lends Minkwitz two thousand gulden.

Dated the Monday after Cantate in 1529.

16. Some articles it is necessary to consider because of the present rapid progress. [May–July] 1529.[68] An opinion about the Evangelical league to be concluded.[69]

First, *since the previous diet of 1529 resulted in a dispute* in which the greater part of the electors, princes, and estates wanted to remain with the old customs devised by people, and held and believed that what was written and prescribed by the ancient fathers is Christian and right, *and therefore declared the conclusions of previous diets regarding the instructions of the emperor to be invalid; since,* however, the other side . . . which at this time was the smallest part, did not want to remain with human precepts and ordinances, but only with the clear and bright Word of God, which can tolerate no human teaching, and resolved that they would obey and be obedient to God more than men, *and therefore would remain with the departure instructions from Speyer, the result was a protest. We can expect nothing good from our enemies; it is to be feared* that they will produce and carry out many wicked tricks in order to remove and drive us away from our lands and people and completely wipe us out. *Now, since* these kings, electors,

67 Handwritten draft . Reg. E. fol. 37a, No. 81, Bl. 235f.

68 A comparison of this with the "Schwabach Correspondence" (PC 1:414f.) and the instructions of the Saxon and Brandenburg councilors for the Schwabach meeting (J. J. Müller, 281f.) reveals that the recommendations of the prince were not overlooked. At any rate, these recommendations were made before the Diet of Schwabach planned for August 9, probably even before the Diet of Rotach (beginning of June), where there was no reference at all to their conclusions. It is interesting that in John Frederick's record, nothing is to be found of the religious qualifications for entrance into the league, which are present in the instructions Müller has.

69 John Frederick's record in his own hand; Reg. H., 10 L, fol. 75f.; used on p. 78 <73>; Ranke 3:117.

princes, and estates are not the lord or government over our side, and were not placed by God as the government over our people, but our side is equal to them in all government and jurisdiction, and thus our side <123> is no less electors, princes, and estates of the empire than they are; since, then, our side is as obliged by God as they are to defend ourselves against unjust violence; accordingly, it follows that our side is obliged before God to administer justice and provide protection and defense of its subjects against those, both subjects and government, who would force them with the sword away from the divine Word.

Because we protested against the article about help against the Turks and therefore, if the Turks should march through Poland, Silesia, and Lusatia, we expect no help from the other estates, it is necessary in these two points to take up the following articles: (1) God is to be asked from the pulpit for peace. If the opponents of His Word, whether they are Papists or Turks, cause strife, then may God grant us the common sense, wisdom, etc., to oppose them. (2) If we have to consider attacking people, that we can be cautious and not be rash.

We take up the first point, *that the estates of the empire that want to adhere to the divine Word should unite so that, if one is invaded, it will be helped in every cost and injury with all might and ability*, so that this is reconciled in two ways, first with rapid help and then with complete help with all might that lasts and continues.

The best way to provide such rapid help is to prescribe privately and discreetly a leader who must be a prince who has the sense for this and is not given to bluster, who is appointed and prescribed for a year; when the year is up, he is allowed to continue if he has the aptitude or another is appointed who is somewhat more desirable. Six councilors of war must be appointed for him, namely, three of electoral and princely stock, one from the counts, and two from the estates, one from the South German estates and the other from the Saxon estates. The leader is not to be hindered from acting by them; the leader is permitted always to have two of his councilors with him as a council of war, but they do not have a vote.

The prince who is made leader over the army must be provided with money (the quantity to be determined, not too much or large), so that he can carry out the business prescribed for him everywhere throughout the empire and in other lands that are attacked. If the leader should happen to hear a report about the Turks that seems to be the tumult and business of war, then the burden for our side is on him that <124> the prince who is the leader demand that the six councilors of war point out the implications of this news, and he should listen to their council and advice.

Now, so that this can happen without any rashness, it would be good if enough money was on deposit for ten thousand soldiers and two thousand cavalry for two months. This should come from the electors and princes of Saxony, Brandenburg, and Hesse, together with the Frankish and other local counts. Their quota should be on deposit in Coburg, and that of the South German estates in Nuremberg. The other princes, such as Osnabrück, Prince Philip of Brunswick, Prince Ernst of Lüneburg, Prince Heinrich of Mecklenburg, Prince Wolff of Anhalt, and the Saxon counts should deposit their money together with the Saxon estates at Magdeburg or Brunswick or wherever else is proper.

Now, if the leader summons the council of war and receives the advice that haste is required in taking up the defense, then the leader should have the authority together with the council of war to prescribe that the money that is on deposit be taken and used for the ten thousand soldiers and two thousand cavalry.

The leader together with the council of war should also have the authority to write for rapid help from the princes, counts, and cities and to summon a number of soldiers from each according to their ability; since this demand comes from the leader, he should be given obedience and compliance.

After calling up and enlisting the soldiers, the leader should also summon the princes, counts, and estates to a specific place suitable for peace, and deliberate with them how, in the case of need, a large and firm defense is to be undertaken.

If the leader and the council of war find that defense is not so urgent, they should first summon the princes, etc., to a deliberation, so that they may most diligently seek peace.

They must also deliberate about how the cannons are to be brought up for speedy help, so that the princes, etc., can move in their cannons.

The leader and the council of war must be paid for their time of service. Some knights and captains over the cavalry must be retained at half-pay, so that they can keep perhaps two thousand cavalry in readiness. *Some of the estates on our side must also be obliged to make an exception in the appointments they receive. The same thing must be done for the captains of the soldiers, since they must keep perhaps eight thousand soldiers on hand.*

Furthermore, it would be good for the electors, princes, counts, and estates each to provide themselves according to their might and ability with cavalry, soldiers, <125> and cannons, together with all that goes with it, and money, provisions, captains, grooms, and other things connected with war, and record each one's ability for attacking—how strong and firm the defense can be and how long it can be maintained.

After some estates have made their position on the protest clear, namely, that they are completely on our side, they are without a doubt to be admitted to this business without difficulty; they must deal with the other estates as they can, and yield to our understanding.

After those from Constance, St. Gall, and other estates that are united with the Swiss Confederation have joined the protest, it seems good for them to act together, once they have embraced the Word of God and joined our understanding.

In addition, it is thought necessary to bring some into this union in secret, namely, the new king of Denmark together with the maritime countries, as far as that can be accomplished. We need to deal more with some, namely, with the king of Poland, the elector of Cologne, the Count Palatinate, the electors, the princes of Jülich and Cleves, Prince Friedrich von Liegnitz, the prince of Pomerania, and others, who can be partially brought in with divine help. They can be admitted to the union with body and goods; it would be good for them to tolerate and help one another. Otherwise, they can be taken away from our opponents in expectation, humanly speaking, that deprived of these brave people, our opponents will accomplish less in the war.

Since no one can know what course the war will take, we must be prepared for a defeat and deal with some cities with which the princes, etc., who adhere to the divine Word have an opening, so that cavalry and soldiers can be marched there, namely, Nuremberg, Ulm, Strasburg of the South German cities, and for the Saxon cities Brunswick, Magdeburg, and Hildesheim, etc.

It would also be necessary to deal with some counts, such as Count Wilhelm and Count Bertolt from Henneberg, Count Jorgen from Wertheim, the count of Schwartzenburg, Heideck, and the other counts of Franconia.

The counts on the Rhine and the Netherland counts have a great confederation with one another, such as Nassau, Hanau, Königstein, Solms, Isenburg, Neuenahr, Westerburg, Manderscheid, Mörs, Reiffenberg, and many more, with whom dealings must be undertaken, as is further to be considered.

<126> Since there were previous dealings to reach an understanding with some Bohemian lords, these should be considered further, such as Rosenberg, Pernstein, Schlick, Hasenstein, Schirow, and others.

The prince chosen as leader needs to confer with the council of war and other people who need to be consulted about what should be done further.

The leader and the council of war should appoint an order of war, and when that has been firmly established, the leader should retain it as needed.

The union established with these and others must be appointed for a year, and not be regarded as a perpetual union.

May God grant His divine grace to all these things. Amen.

17. Thoughts about how our gracious lord, the elector of Saxony, can lessen the burden on His Electoral Grace's land. *[May–July] 1529.*[70]

First, as in the previous list,[71] the people in the principality should be admonished to ask God for grace.

Next, because of the great need, the court should always be provided with good advisors for the difficult matters and new business that comes up each day; therefore, it is advisable that there should not be less than eight advisors at court so that difficult matters may be attended to and justice quickly shown to the poor.

Since His Electoral Grace is now maintaining two courts at Torgau and Weimar, the advisors who can be used in Weimar are not always at Torgau, and vice versa; accordingly, a distinction needs to be made between who is used at each court and who is appointed for the other place.

Those used at Torgau are:

The master of Lichtenberg
Hans von Minkwitz
Hans von der Planitz, or
Hans von Weissenbach
Gunter von Bunau at Altenburg
Hans Metzsch
Dietrich von Starschedel
Benedict Pauli
Caspar von Minkwitz

Those used at Weimar are:

von Wildenfels
Friedrich Thun
Wolff von Weissenbach
Ludwig von Boyneburg
Nicolas von Ende
Christoph von der Planitz
Elwald von Brandstein
Doctor von den Saxon

<127> In addition, there are daily court speeches,[72] with Christoph von Taubenheim, Doctor Brück, Hans von Dolzig, or Doctor Christianus as the preacher.

Wherever His Electoral Grace's court is, it is honorably and necessarily provided with these councilors.

His Electoral Grace needs to put in place an order so that the councilors who must be taken from one place to another are informed about the secret

---

70 John Frederick's list in his own hand. Reg. H., 10, L. fol. 81–84; used on pp. 62 <53>, 78 <73>.

71 That is, Official Document No. 16; see p. 124 <122>.

72 Cf. Burkhardt, *Landtagsakten*, 1:220.

matters, so that when there is a need for defense, His Electoral Grace can know what is necessary quickly, namely, that the counts and knights are kept in readiness and the tithe is paid, how many mounted horses His Electoral Grace can muster quickly, and further that the estates and ministry, the counts and knights will provide foot soldiers.

Because the peasants have no experience with war, soldiers are accepted in their place, as the estates and the ministry together with the counts and the knights can provide people in their place supported by the tax on the common people, so that the money is deposited for use.

There should further be reflection on the order for making a supply depot among the estates and ministry and with the counts and nobility, in which each according to ability could deposit something to be used when there is need, and if this is done for a year or more, as long as God grants peace, it can be hoped to have a large amount of grain and other things in the land.

This can be used in two ways: first, in war; second, in peace when there is famine—which may God graciously prevent!—the poor can purchase this for little money in the estates and ministry and the subjects of the counts and nobility can be helped; the money from this can be deposited for war; if there is peace, money can be laid aside in good years, and the surplus again be sold.

If the military comes into the land, we must also look at whether we can advise something better. We must consider how to provide for the cannons and all they need, and the councilors must pay attention to what is not present but is needed.

Since the court at Weimar is completely unprotected except by cannons, we should consider where and how to place the cannons so that there is no harm to the court.

<128> The councilors must consider having whatever else is necessary and belongs to the war in readiness, so that it can be commanded and decreed by His Electoral Grace.

The region will also have to be arranged; therefore, we should consider, when the court is at Torgau, appointing a leader at Doringen—as this is presently being arranged by Prince George—who can quickly, before danger comes to Torgau, carry out the decrees and further commands of His Electoral Grace.

For this purpose, we should employ von Wildenfels, and the council of war should also appoint Ludwig von Boyneburg, Nicolas von Ende, and Konrad Gotzmann.

In Voitland, Wolff von Weissenbach should be commissioned to have supervision of the other magistrates.

It will be necessary to appoint a guardian for Coburg, and someone else to have oversight; we should consider employing for these matters Hans von Scherrenberg and Gotzmann, if von Wildenfels does not require Gotzmann.

If something happens in the electorate of Saxony, we can order Count Albrecht von Mansfeld who has Allstadt to take care of it, and provide him as a council of war Hans von Minkwitz and Hans Metzsch, commander at Wittenberg.

These councilors should have governance of the war over all magistrates, so that everything can be employed quickly.

Further, it is necessary to provide for master gunners, who will be difficult enough to find when we need them.

After the first few cavalry have come into the land in force, it will be highly necessary to seek someone who can be trusted to act and remain completely under His Electoral Grace, such as Jost von Steinberg or another who is qualified for this position.

We should take counsel what Jost von Steinberg should receive if he is called upon to act courageously.

It would also be good to have at least two hundred horses kept in readiness at court; if something happened, they would be more useful than four hundred elsewhere. If there is a problem with the cost, some unnecessary domestic servants can be discharged or employed on other matters.

Since His Electoral Grace's land has not been provided with fortification, other than Wittenberg, it is recommended that His Electoral Grace fortify two other places, such as Coburg castle, which will be easy at little cost, and then another <129> place in the land at Döringen, wherever is considered best, whether Gotha or elsewhere. This can be done with the help of the peasantry, so that His Electoral Grace does not have such a large cost for it, especially if the castle at Gotha is chosen along with the monastery.

It is good to remember that Erfurt is completely within the electorate, as His Electoral Grace confesses before his liege lords and princes that they should consider fitting ways to guard the roads, so that with divine help, an opening is achieved when necessary and there are casualties in the land—which may God graciously prevent—Erfurt would then be a fortified place in the midst of the land; it is to be hoped that from such a fortified place, a whole land that has been lost may be regained.

18. July 22, 1529, letter from Prince John Frederick to Count Wilhelm von Neuenahr. Answer to his letter of July 8.[73] Family news, the Nassau controversy, Philip von Solms, the courtship. Joy at the good terms established between Cologne and Saxony at the diet. Visit with his parents-in-law. Settlement of Neuenahr's quarrel with Loraine and Geldern. Neuenahr's relationship with Ferdinand. Reports about the Turks. The wedding in Loraine.[74]

Thanks for the letter, family news. I am happy to hear that you have received a report from Hans about my innocence in the Nassau affair. I also hope to God you have found nothing else with both my dear and kind uncles, the margrave and Count Wilhelm von Nassau, for I am glad to see that they are equally inclined on both sides to establish a friendly agreement, which could not be obtained by my diligence. However, the almighty God will still according to His divine will grant success; I will not hesitate to do whatever I can that will help this settlement.

I am glad to hear you have received knowledge of what I commanded Count Philip von Solms to point out to my uncle, Count Wilhelm von Nassau, with the knowledge of my gracious lord and father, for I know that you will much more promote this than hinder it. However, I must complain that I still have not received an answer to my good wishes to them, which I meant in a faithful and friendly way; I cannot imagine what reasons there may be.[75]

<130> I will further command Hans with an offer regarding your person that for my sake, he would seek from you something new, also some cavalry equipment, that you would report as I have hoped. I know that I will command Hans to remember and act with special grace according to your thoughts, that you would ask what it depends on, with the result that you would ask me in writing.

However, because by God's grace, the matters tend, as you reported, to happen to our advantage, we thank the almighty God that by His divine will, He has turned these and other things for the best, also those difficulties that happened on our side for the best, so that our side is not in a rush. The course that Count Felix von Werdenberg has taken with other leaders of the imperial majesty has been for the best; may God grant the imperial majesty and his

73 Cornelius 10:155f.

74 Draft in his own hand. Loc. 10671 "Schreiben und Bedenken," fol. 34–37.

75 This probably refers to the planned marriage of Wilhelm with Princess Marie.

people success, so that the imperial majesty carries it out well and achieves peace with their adversaries.

I am very glad to hear that my lord and friend from Cologne had a friendly conference with my gracious lord and father, the elector of Saxony, and reached an agreement. God and you are to be thanked that it has come this far, and if God graciously grants that they are together more, I will hope that they will continue in friendly agreement.

I certainly desire to journey to Jülich and Cleves to catch up on news, *if I can get away from my father. I do not dare to come without an invitation; perhaps you can arrange that.*

I am glad to hear that your business with the princes of Loraine and Geldern is proceeding, and want you to know that I rejoice at your welfare as if it were my own.

I do not envy you for what happened to you with the king of Bohemia, but when you confess God's Word before the world, you must also suffer persecution for it; one is better than the other, namely, that you must suffer something for Christ's sake and be accused of being a heretic.

I will share some news with you about the Turks: as far as I can tell, the victories are completely certain and are ascribed to a prince who was appointed and sworn in as leader and used against the Turks because of the empire; <131> similarly, there was a mutual settlement with the Swiss.

Since I also note from your letter that the prince of Loraine is again in the grace of the imperial majesty, I desire to know whether the imperial majesty is once again displeased and has difficulties with the Loraine marriage with my wife's sister. Accordingly, I desire that when you next write to me, you would tell me the situation and whether you expect that the marriage will soon be consummated. In addition, I ask that if you come across something else you think I should know, that you would let me know this. . . . Dated at Torgau on the day of Mary Magdalene 1529.

---

19. December 18, 1529, letter from Prince John Frederick at Torgau to Wolf von Schönberg, magistrate at Meissen. In keeping with Wolf's proposal, he is ready to seek together with his cousin John a settlement of the dispute between their fathers.[76]

When you next come to Torgau for the nuptials of our doorman, the faithful Wolf von Rascha, your brother-in-law, since it seemed good to you to give

---

76 Final draft in Reg. A. 242. Used on p. 63 <54>.

advice in this matter of the differences between our dear and gracious lord and father on the one hand and our dear cousin Prince George of Saxony on the other hand, it was your opinion that nothing better could be done than that we follow your advice on this. Although it seemed foolish to me to seek this, yet it is clear that you meant it well; if our cousin Prince John is inclined to confer on this, it will not be difficult to meet with him. It was your opinion that if we achieved this with our cousin, His Grace would have no difficulty with it. The result between us two on this matter was that we should reflect on this further and that if we found that we and our cousin should consider this matter, then we would write to you so that you could propose this to His Grace, and if you found that His Grace approved of this, then His Grace could set a date for our meeting and prescribe how we should confer with each other. We do not want to conceal from you that we have not neglected your submissive advice <132> to consider the matter; as previously noted, we still intend nothing else than that our lord and father would agree with our cousin Prince George on all their differences; so we desire Your Grace, when you next come to Torgau, to propose this to our cousin Prince John and inquire whether, if we bring all these matters to our two fathers, they will discuss them in a friendly way. If His Grace would let us know if he is inclined to do this or not, then we will immediately let you know this by writing with our own hands; if you can carry out these things soon with submissive good intentions, we will show you our gracious good pleasure. Dated at Torgau on the Saturday evening after St. Luke in the year of our Lord 1529.

20. October 8, 1530, letter from Prince John Frederick at Torgau to Princess Elisabeth of Saxony. Thanks for her October 5 letter. The alleged intrigues of Prince George to obtain feudal tenure in the principality. Defense of his actions in Augsburg. Negotiations there about the monastery estates. Defense of his actions toward his father. Explanation that he did not cause the discord, but the cause is to be sought in Prince George. Pills against pestilence. Luther's four evangelists and prophets.[77]

Today I received your writing dated the Wednesday after St. Michael's Day. After reading your friendly remarks, I perceive nothing else than that you mean them well. I do appreciate your thoughts about what is of first concern,

77 Draft in his own hand. Reg. A. 241. Used on pp. 56 <47>, 63 <54>.

namely, what to advise my cousin Prince George of Saxony to do in order to obtain as a fief from his imperial majesty the electorate of Saxony. I want to tell you that I heard nothing especially believable about this at Augsburg; I also do not expect that he will undertake this, since this would be opposed to the sworn and pledged inheritance. Rather, he is much more obliged to promote rather than hinder the good of my gracious lord and father.

The other thing I note from your writing is that you fault me for defending in Augsburg when people do not adopt what is not against Scripture but serves for peace and unity. This should only be done in the self-interest of the spiritual goods, and if this is the case, <133> they should not relinquish this principle. I have to point out that those who told you this gave you a makeshift report or intentionally misrepresented things. If you heard everything that was discussed on all the articles about faith, conscience, and abuse, you would find that the matter of self-interest or the convent estates was not pushed, but that we discussed the matters that God and conscience will not allow, which will come to light at the proper time. It is a true report that when I was at Augsburg, his imperial majesty did not mention what should be done with regard to the article about the convent estates. When the imperial majesty's articles, which replaced our articles, were read, the convent estates were not mentioned. Third, when the committee of fourteen persons discussed this article, it was not mentioned either. After the departure of Prince Heinrich of Brunswick,[78] my cousin Prince George of Saxony came to the committee with good will toward my gracious lord and father and the rest of us; he immediately called forth the articles on the convents and proposed that they be discussed, since discussing these and other things would destroy the other discussions. Accordingly, it is not proper to impose on me that I hindered something that could have happened with God and conscience and served peace. If you can point out to me in truth that I did yield more of what was imposed on me by our side than I should have, I hope that you will find us innocent and not with too much injustice, for if you hear what we sought in the matter of the convents, you will find that we did not seek our own self-interest, but yielded everything we could before God and conscience.

Third, what my gracious lord and father has imposed on me toward you, namely, how I should act toward His Grace and how he will rule, etc., of which I am innocent, I must let happen and submit to God, for we cannot shut every untruthful mouth, but they lie as much as they want. Whoever is here, or

---

78 On this journey, see Schirrmacher, 212; it took place on August 18 (CR 2:848).

wherever I am with my gracious lord and father, can assess how I act toward him, whether according to the report you received <134> or not; for now, I will leave it there and entrust it to God.

Fourth, I note that they have made a mess at your court because of me, as if I seek everything that serves discord and mutiny, and especially that at my arrival, I do away with what was decided by my gracious lord and father's advisors; I also attack the retinue and tribute and want things to be different from how they have been for forty years. So I will not conceal your friendly view that I cannot be bound enough, from which the people who make things so difficult take their motive, for I find nothing about the retinue and tribute in what I wrote to my cousin Prince Frederick of Saxony from which they could take any motive. I wrote nothing else than this: After I remembered that this was the problem between my gracious lord and father and my cousin Prince George of Saxony for many years and was still not dealt with by the others, in the absence of my gracious lord and father, it was not proper for all kinds of reasons to do anything without his previous knowledge; I wanted to let him know this, and, without doubt, he would regard it as appropriate and not fault it. There will never be a fair reason from this answer to accuse me of seeking provocation and aversion. If what I write is against the old inheritance agreements, even though I did not touch on them with the least word that was against them, except that I could not do anything without my gracious lord and father's foreknowledge, which is not so hard to evaluate or talk about among understanding people, who otherwise love peace and honor and do not seek discord or try to cause that discord for their lord. There is no reason from my writing (God be praised!) for anyone to accuse me with a truthful basis of seeking discord, or that I gave my gracious lord and father or anyone on our side a reason for war and discord. If I were to point out to you that your father and my cousin Prince George forcefully denied my gracious lord and father against what was granted and against the union agreed to, along with denial of the silver gathered in his principality, even though my gracious lord and father distributed his help; with what right was this denied? My cousin asked the imperial majesty to burden and dislodge my gracious lord and father and to oppress him as much as he could, so that our faith <135> and adherence to the holy divine Word would not be unpunished. Even if he were forcefully evicted, so that the silver would be unjustly divided, and this would be done against the fraternal inheritance agreement, which was intended to be faithful and friendly, and then appeal to the imperial majesty to burden him; you can easily realize how this gives a reason for wicked provocation and the shedding of blood! However,

God willing, I do not want to take excessive counsel on distinct reasons for beginning war on our side or just causes for that. My gracious lord and father (God be praised!) has still not been found any different, but will let my cousin Prince George begin, which I do not anticipate happening. We, for our part, appeal to God for help with our righteous cause, since we have given no reason for their antipathy. God willing, we would give war enough, but you should know that it is not my intention, nor is it my gracious lord and father's intention to deprive my cousin of anything proper for him, except that I do not want my gracious lord and father deprived of anything that belongs to him according to the agreement.

Before your letter, I also received one from Hans Spiegel; as far as the pills for pestilence are concerned, which I am to send to you, Hans Spiegel did not tell me anything about what those pills are supposed to be. I will gladly send them when I know what they are and that you will receive them.

I still know nothing about the four evangelists and the prophets, which Dr. Martin is supposed to have published recently, but when I receive them, I will send them to you and not withhold them from you. . . . Dated at Torgau on the Saturday after St. Francis in 1530.

21. October 24, 1530, letter from Prince John Frederick to [Count Wilhelm von Nassau].[79] Defense of the way the Evangelicals acted at the diet.[80]

Dear high-born uncle, I have no doubt that you have by now heard how my gracious lord and father and the rest of us left Augsburg, what happened with God and His divine Word, and without doubt the ill will that led to a difficult and unchristian departure. I have no doubt that you have received a sufficient report about this, <136> and that this has in many ways made our high respect for them difficult, for which my gracious lord and father and I are truly sorry. There was no defect at all on our side (God be praised!) in all that happened with regard to God and conscience, but our opponents had to admit that the confession we handed in is not against God's Word and the Holy Gospel. It was accepted and confirmed as true by those who want to be the Christian Church. We acted as if our consciences were at peace because (God be praised!) we have our own confession, so that our adversaries must leave our confession founded

79 His answer on November 24 makes it clear that he is the addressee here.

80 Draft in his own hand. Reg. E. fol. 37a, No. 88; used on p. 56 <47>.

on God's Word, since they have to honor God and His Word. So we must entrust all of this to God and let Him act; in all humility, we would prefer to have an ungracious emperor rather than an ungracious God. Even though the imperial majesty has the power and ability, granted him by God, to take away our body and property, yet his authority does not extend over our souls; God, however, can take away body, soul, and property and throw them into eternal fire. With His[81] help, we will fear Him more than all secular authority. I can imagine that we have been highly disparaged by our adversaries to you and your brother, also my uncle, in this matter. My request is that you would not believe anything they say in this matter without hearing our answer; if this is reported to your brother, or you hear something to the disparagement of my gracious lord and father and of myself, when we hear about this, we will gladly explain how this disparagement has been unjustly imposed on us. . . . Hurriedly dated in my own hand on Monday, the twenty-fourth day of October in 1530.

22. December 28, 1530, letter from Prince John Frederick at Cologne to Elector John. All kinds of news from Cologne.[82]

I received today Your Grace's writing from Smalcald, and express thanks to Your Grace for your paternal concern for me, my wife, and my children, and I am ready submissively to serve Your Grace.

As things are everywhere, Your Grace will <137> realize from my other writing[83] the way things are here; it is obvious that the kingdom is being miserably surrendered and sold to the king of Bohemia; even though people make fun of the danger of a free election, that is unfortunately the intention.

Frau Margaretha, the queen of the Netherlands, is dead; although the imperial majesty and the king are very sad and wear black, it does not seem that they are very sad within.

The royal robe is ready to be replaced, and everything is ready when we are certain about the matter.

Those who take care of the herons are here and have many thousand gulden; when the work is completed, then the promised reward will follow.

81 A word was blotted out.

82 Handwritten. Loc. 10671 "Concerning the Election of King Ferdinand in 1531." Used on p. 83 <80>; Winckelmann, 69.

83 That is, a detailed report on the election negotiations in "Schreiben und Bedenken," fol. 136–41, original.

The pope has settled on Italy for the council, and the king today agreed with that counsel. The imperial majesty will remain in the empire until the council. Everything is ready for Your Grace and her relatives to hurry and seek more rights than you had. Accordingly, unavoidable necessity demands that the matter not be forgotten, but kept on the alert for defense, as Your Grace thinks best. So I wish for Your Grace from God the Almighty a happy, Christian, good new year. . . . Dated hurriedly in my own hand at Cologne on the Rhine on the Wednesday after Christmas 1531.

23. September 29, 1531, letter from Prince John Frederick at Weimar to Count Wilhelm von Neuenahr. Inquiry about the negotiations with the emperor. Thorough warnings about attending the diet. Note dated at Weimar October 1: advice on the marriage of Wilhelm von Nassau with Princess Marie.[84]

Now that I have received all kinds of information from my uncle Count Wilhelm von Nassau and you about what my gracious lord and father dispatched again to the Roman imperial majesty, I have no doubt that all this was carried out by him and you for the best; here this business must rest, of which my gracious lord and father and I have no knowledge. I can suspect, however, that it is not his or your fault, but there is another reason why no answer has come here. But I will not conceal from you that all kinds of reliable warnings have come to my gracious lord and father and me <138> that we should not rely on getting by with a visit to the diet by His Grace or me, for there is disturbing danger and difficulty there, etc. Although I do not know what you and my uncle have done with the articles to which my gracious lord and father agreed with regard to attending the diet himself or through me, I did want to point out to you that these many important warnings concern me not a little; if I must attend the diet to agree with these articles, then I will greatly rely on my uncle Count Wilhelm and you. Even though he and you have worked carefully at court as you know best, there is still concern about unfaithfulness; so you will not let me remain unforewarned, since I rely on him and you for everything good. . . . Dated at Weimar on the Friday after St. Michael 1531.

Note (ibid., fol. 94), October 1 at Weimar.

In addition, I do not doubt that you know how for some time now, I have spoken with you about whether my uncle Count Wilhelm von Nassau and my

84 Draft in his own hand. Reg. H., 50, No. 5, fol. 89/90, 94; used on pp. 77 <73>, 88 <85>.

sister should get married; I see that my uncle Count Wilhelm is somewhat willing that I, who am inclined to Count Wilhelm for all reasons of friendship, should diligently promote him to my gracious lord and father and that sister of mine who pleases him. However, I have never been able to grasp Count Wilhelm's nature other than that he is far too old to marry, where I have so far let it rest. But I will not conceal from you that when I asked my gracious lord and father about my sister, and about other people who do not matter, my gracious lord and father stopped me after I had determined that on both sides, my uncle Count Wilhelm and my sister, there was a special inclination to this and to no other. Accordingly, I have told you this and desire that you would explore my uncle Count Wilhelm's intentions about this after he has seen my sister; let me know what you find out. If he wishes, he will find me a friend and faithful intercessory. . . . Dated at Weimar on the Sunday after Michaelmas in 1530 [1531].

<139> 24. May 7, 1532, letter from Prince John Frederick at Schweinfurt to Elector John. Report on the final negotiations in Schweinfurt. Request to invite the theologians to a consultation in Wittenberg on the evening of the thirteenth.[85]

I will be in Torgau on Sunday or Monday. The way things have begun, I have some hope that as far as religion is concerned, things will reach the good goal of Christian peace. *The final negotiation took place on Wednesday. A new diet will be held in Nuremberg, and the electors are to submit to the imperial majesty the means on which we agreed Wednesday* . . . so, I think it necessary for Your Grace to have the final decision of the theologians at Wittenberg heard, and if there is the opportunity, to present all the articles thoroughly. It is my opinion and request that Your Grace would summon Doctor Martin, Pomeranus if he is still in Wittenberg, Philip, and Jonas to come to Torgau next Monday evening so that their views on such very important matters are heard, whether the articles are acceptable to them before God and conscience or not; then we could finally decide to remain with these articles and set the proper course. . . . Dated at Schweinfurt on the Tuesday of Vocem Jocunditatis toward evening, 1532.

85 Original. Reg. H. No. 16, vol. 3, fol. 109; used on pp. 58 <49>, 90 <88>.

25. June 21, 1532, letter from Prince John Frederick at Nuremberg to Elector John. Request that the theologians give their opinion on the peace negotiations. Belzig's mission along the Danube.[86]

Answer to two letters from June 11. The Erfurt business. Report that the negotiations in Nuremberg are still not very promising. My opinion about all this business that has taken place these days, of which I sent copies to Your Grace, especially because the theologians and scholars on our side here are very opposed to one another, is that Your Grace should prevail on Dr. Martin Luther and the other scholars at Wittenberg to give Your Grace further thoughts on this. When this happens, Your Grace could forward that to me . . . so that I and my fellows could act all the better according to it.

I will send you a copy of why I sent Albrecht of Belzig to Vienna, Pressburg, and Moravia to investigate about the Turks and survey the opportunities and necessities. <140> *New intelligence from Venice about the Turks.*

26. July 5, 1532, letter from Hans von Minkwitz in Torgau to Prince John Frederick. Information about the Turks. The meeting planned between John Frederick and the landgrave. Report on the committee at Zwickau. The journey of the electoral princess. Gifts to Luther and the elector. Georg Späte. The fortification of Wittenberg. Note about the payments of Ernst von Brunswick. Health of the elector.[87]

At the command of Your Princely Grace, I will go next Monday and report to my lord.

With difficulty, I have obtained information from Poland, Prussia, Silesia, Lusatia, etc., that the leader from Hersberg is ready to do everything, no matter what is believed about the advance of the Turks and other unchristian people.

His Electoral Grace is very pleased with the meeting between Your Princely Grace and the landgrave at Smalcald. So His Electoral Grace did not challenge the approach of the servant or Your Princely Grace's writing to the leaders, but only thinks this should be done cautiously, so that the landgrave does not make a tumult.

---

86 Rough draft. Reg. H., 65, No. 17, vol. 2, fol. 42–44; used on p. 58 <50>.

87 Handwritten. Reg. A. 247; used on pp. 38f. <27>.

The XII decreed for the region is set for Zwickau on the Sunday after Margaret, as Your Princely Grace undoubtedly knows. All other articles, which Your Princely Grace wanted investigated for Silesia and included in my instructions,[88] will have to wait until the leader from Hersberg comes or writes.

The articles that Nicolas von End and Hans Metzsch are to prepare are also not in place, for my gracious lord will not summon Nicolas von End and will not let Hans Metzsch travel to him, although it is common sense that this is good and necessary, and he has been reminded of this three times.

My gracious lord is pleased with the journey of Your Princely Grace's wife, my gracious prince, the young lord, and Your Princely Grace's servants, etc.; he has also agreed for you to send or write that my gracious lord should provide for them.

His Electoral Grace will write to the steward at Coburg and send a list of what Your Princely Grace should requisition from the district and otherwise buy, and order some other things from here and Weimar. <141> Moreover, His Electoral Grace has written to the stewards at Voitsberg and Arnshaug to have the fodder follow Your Princely Grace, namely, that the steward at Voitsberg provide fifteen casks of diminished fodder and the steward at Arnshaug fifty half-tons of undiminished fodder.

I have not been able to file the letters, but the articles will be delayed until Your Princely Grace's arrival. I have answered Your Princely Grace's letter to my gracious wife, and thereby made the best report about Your Princely Grace; Your Princely Grace's people were also notified of the journey with the foreknowledge of my gracious lord; some were happy, but some were sad. I sent Doctor Martin Your Princely Grace's gift with a letter, but have not yet received an answer.

I have also submissively delivered the gems to my gracious lord, which His Electoral Grace kindly accepted from Your Princely Grace, but I cannot tell whether His Electoral Grace will keep the gems or not.

I have not been able to accomplish anything in the matter of Georg Späte, but I do note that my gracious lord will allow Your Princely Grace along with the wife at Franconia to support him; I informed Späte, and he and his wife will journey with my gracious prince.

The building at Wittenberg is proceeding; my gracious lord recently ordered five hundred florins for it. I will be there myself, God willing, in a few days and speak with the captain about the moat and other things, as Your Princely Grace

---

88 Reg. H., 65, No. 17, vol. 2, fol. 57–66, draft.

commanded. . . . Hurriedly in my own hand at Torgau on the Friday after the Visitation of Mary 1532.

Note: I submissively tell Your Princely Grace that my gracious lord, Count Ernst, yesterday gave 4,872 florins, which His Princely Grace values at twenty-five groschen per gulden; my gracious lord would not receive the money, but commanded me to receive it and apply it to Coburg. Accordingly, it will be kept in custody, God willing, until Your Princely Grace's command or arrival. His Princely Grace has once again written about the deposit and asked my gracious lord to hinder that until it is needed, but my gracious lord insists on his previous answer and renews it, as Your Princely Grace considered at Nuremberg and His Electoral Grace prescribed.

It is so droll here that I could wish I was with Your Princely Grace at Nuremberg. My gracious lord's foot has healed, but His Electoral Grace cannot walk and, as people say, it is worse to step on his good leg than on his bad one. His Electoral Grace has gone on the hunt several times and again yesterday, but he must be carried to the carriage and back from it. Dated submissively.

27. July 9, 1532, letter from Prince John Frederick at Nuremberg to Elector John. No one agrees with the opinion of Luther and Jonas. Negotiations with both electors. <142> Aversion of the Hessian councilors to the peace. First note: Propaganda. Second note: Recommendation to prohibit the export of grain.[89]

News about the proposals of both electors on July 4. Although Your Grace sent me, along with Doctor Martin and the provost at Wittenberg,[90] further thoughts touching on the articles of the imperial majesty, as if these articles ought to be approved, not one of my friends, nor of the margrave, nor those of Nuremberg, even those very lenient in this business, think these articles can be accepted without insult to the divine glory.

I with the others have undertaken some necessary improvements in the proposals of the two electors, and I am forwarding these improvements to them. They have made some additions to them, and on Sunday, sent the articles to the emperor. Now, even if the emperor should not approve the words added about putting an end to the legal proceedings, I still think that we should accept the articles as they were submitted by the electors on Thursday [the fourth], even though . . . the landgrave's councilors are against it, for in my

89 Original. Reg. H., 65, No. 17, vol. 3, fol. 58–60; used on pp. 59 <51>, 92f. <91>; Winckelmann, 233, 236.

90 Justus Jonas. The thoughts are found in WA Br 6:323.

opinion, they would prefer to break the peace rather than establish it, for there have been somewhat harsh disputations between me together with my cousin Count Francis and them. However, I think that if the Nassau affair is included in the peace, he will agree with what is right, and the dealings with him will not be difficult.

The emperor's quarrels with the estates at Regensburg. The danger from the Turks. Personalities. . . . Dated at Nuremberg on the Tuesday after Kilian in the year of our Lord 1532.

First note (fol. 61f). Preparation for war. It is recommended that the assembled servants spend some time with weapons, which will be harder to do later.

Second note (fol. 63f). Recommendation to renew the prohibition of the export of grain because of the dangerous times. The South German cities complain especially about the great stripping away of their reserves of grain; a great famine is to be feared also for other reasons. We must anticipate that. We must also impress on both the lords of Gera, the count at Schwarzburg, etc., the importance of the prohibition, and write to their officials.

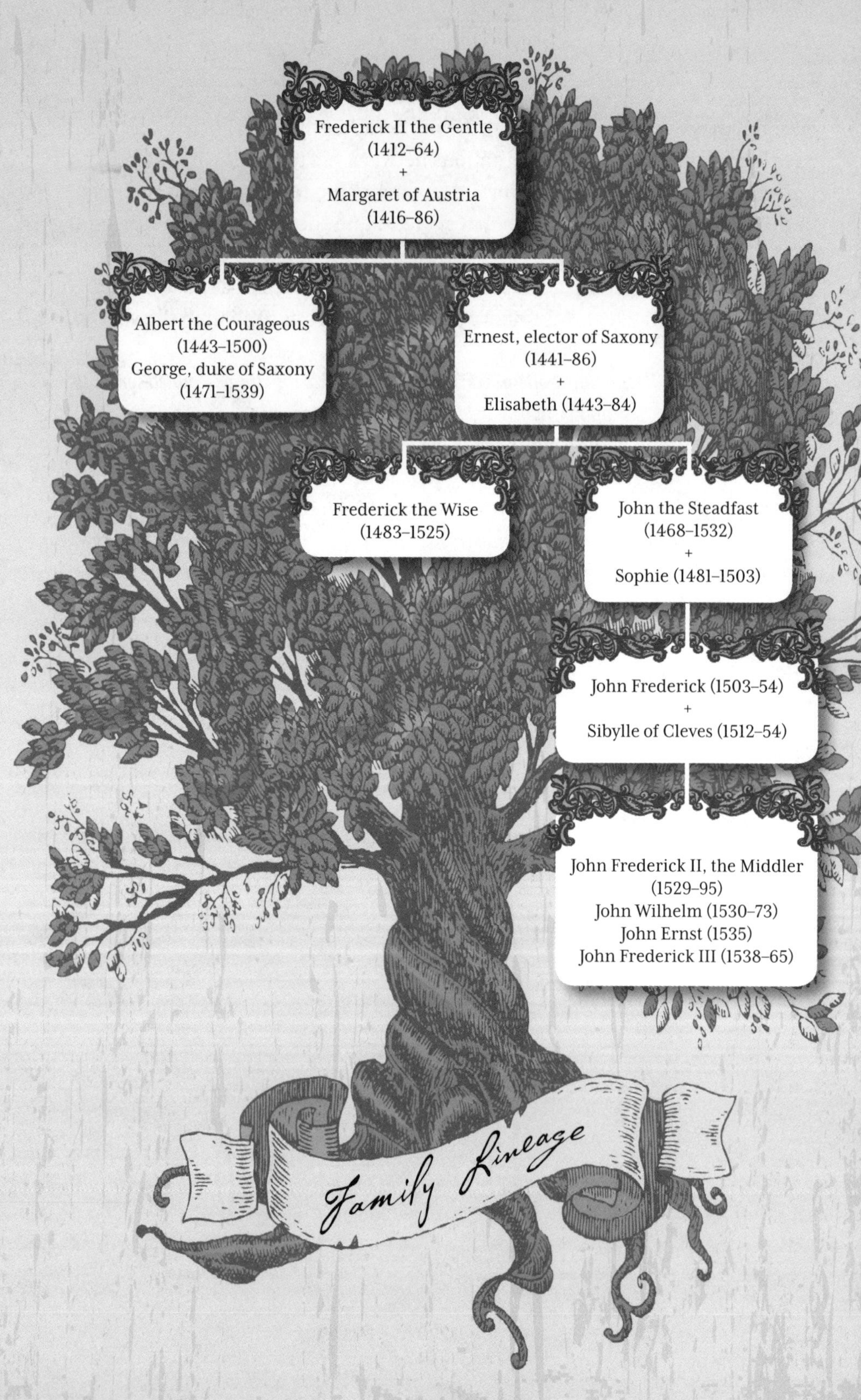
Frederick II the Gentle
(1412–64)
+
Margaret of Austria
(1416–86)
Albert the Courageous
(1443–1500)
George, duke of Saxony
(1471–1539)
Ernest, elector of Saxony
(1441–86)
+
Elisabeth (1443–84)
Frederick the Wise
(1483–1525)
John the Steadfast
(1468–1532)
+
Sophie (1481–1503)
John Frederick (1503–54)
+
Sibylle of Cleves (1512–54)
John Frederick II, the Middler
(1529–95)
John Wilhelm (1530–73)
John Ernst (1535)
John Frederick III (1538–65)
Family Lineage